WHAT ABOUT Spiritual Warfare?

WHAT ABOUT
Spiritual Warfare?

Douglas J. Rumford

TYNDALE HOUSE PUBLISHERS, INC. | WHEATON, ILLINOIS

Visit Tyndale's exciting Web site at www.tyndale.com

Designed by Justin Ahrens.

Published in association with the literary agency of Alive Communications, Inc., 7680 Goddard Street, Suite 200, Colorado Springs, CO 80920.

People's names and certain details of the stories in this book have been changed to protect the privacy of the individuals involved. However, the facts of what happened and the underlying principles have been conveyed as accurately as possible.

A significant portion of the material in chapter 7 was adapted from an article the author wrote titled "Lead Us Out of Temptation" that was first published in *New Man* magazine, January/February 1997.

Library of Congress Cataloging-in-Publication Data

Rumford, Douglas J.
    What about spiritual warfare? / Douglas J. Rumford.
        p. cm.
    Includes bibliographical references.
    ISBN 0-8423-7404-3 (pbk.)
        1. Spiritual warfare.   2. Demonology.   3. Sin.   I. Title

BV4509.5 .R85 2000
235'.4—dc21   00-023423

Printed in the United States of America

06   05   04   03   02   01   00
7   6   5   4   3   2   1

CONTENTS

CHAPTER ONE: 1
Are We Really in a Spiritual War?

CHAPTER TWO: 15
Seeing the World through Different Eyes

CHAPTER THREE: 25
Meet the Enemies

CHAPTER FOUR: 41
Where Victory Begins

CHAPTER FIVE: 53
Know Your Weapons

CHAPTER SIX: 71
The Ultimate Weapon—Prayer

CHAPTER SEVEN: 93
Battling Temptation

CHAPTER EIGHT: 107
Confronting the Powers of Darkness

CHAPTER NINE: 127
Holy Battle Strategies

CHAPTER ONE

Are We Really in a Spiritual War?

I need to tell you right up front—before we tackle a subject that some people think is kind of "weird"—that I am a pretty "normal" person. In fact, I think I am probably pretty much like you. I grew up in a middle-class American town, went through public education, played sports, got married, and had a family. I am also what you would classify as a pretty ordinary follower of Jesus Christ. You wouldn't call me a fanatic. I have prayed through my prayer lists, done my quiet times, and shared my faith with others when they seemed receptive. I have followed in the mainstream of twentieth-century evangelical theology, affirming that the Bible is the Word of God, totally true and trustworthy. I believe Jesus Christ died for our sins and that we must believe in him to have eternal life.

For the most part, I have been a pretty normal pastor. I attended seminary and have been a minister for over twenty years in a traditional, historic Protestant denomination. I guess what I am trying to say is that I fit the mold of what many think of as an average person. That's why my experience with Jim and Cheryl was so unsettling.

Cheryl had been battling cancer for several years. She and her husband had gone to a number of healing services and reported their experiences back to me. On one occasion, a pastor well known for his ministry in "signs and wonders" told them that Cheryl was demonized and that I, as her home pastor, should pray for her deliverance. I can't quite express the mix of feelings that swirled inside when Jim and Cheryl came to my study at church and said, "Doug, we've run out of medical options. Our only hope is that the Lord might use you as part of Cheryl's deliverance and healing."

There is a huge difference between theological reflection and looking into the faces of a couple who are literally wrestling with life and death. I have often prayed with others for healing. I believe in the existence of the devil. But until Jim and Cheryl came to see me, I had never been confronted with a situation in which I had to decide what I really believed about demons and deliverance.

The day that Jim and Cheryl asked me to participate in praying for Cheryl's deliverance, I assured them of my commitment to them and to following the Lord's leading. I said I would pray, study God's Word, and seek counsel as I tried to figure out how best to proceed. Then I asked our associate pastor, Chuck, to join me for prayer with them before they left.

Cheryl was seated in a chair and we knelt around her.

I was in front of her. As we began to pray, Cheryl began to cough. It was as if she were choking.

"It's moving," she said.

I opened my eyes and saw her pointing to a marble-sized lump near her collarbone. We could actually see it rolling under her skin across a several-inch region just below her neck. Each time we started praying, Cheryl would cough.

"There was a similar reaction when John Wimber, founder of the Vineyard [a Christian movement that emphasizes God's power evidenced through miraculous signs and wonders such as healing and deliverance], prayed for us," said Jim. "We'll take that as a good sign."

As we continued to pray, I spoke a word of command—by faith, although not conviction—that the "interference" cease immediately. It did! Cheryl seemed comforted by our prayer. As she and Jim left, however, I felt as though my spiritual comfort level was about to be challenged.

I didn't understand what was happening, but one thing I knew: I didn't feel powerful. And I didn't feel ready for this sort of ministry. Besides wondering whether I had just encountered a demon of some sort, I had many preconceptions that this sort of work was for those much more holy and bold than I was.

After that experience, Jim and Cheryl entered dark days. Cheryl's condition deteriorated rapidly. She was hospitalized, and the look of death came upon her. But her husband hung on—relentless in his faith and in his determination to do everything possible to enable Cheryl's healing. In the meantime, I was reading the

Bible and relevant books, praying, thinking, and talking about spiritual warfare with people I trusted. I still couldn't imagine that I would ever be directly confronting personal forces of evil—that is, demons—but I was beginning to notice how much of Jesus' ministry was directed against Satan's kingdom. I was also learning about the authority that believers have in Christ, so that we need not fear evil.

Several months later, we decided to have a special prayer time for Cheryl at her home. Two other pastors joined me there. As we prayed, Cheryl began to tremble and shake. This was especially disconcerting since she was so weakened by her illness and cancer treatments. Keith, a pastor with some experience in praying for deliverance from demonization, called on the spirit that was apparently affecting Cheryl to make itself known. It said, "I am."

"You are what? Who are you?"

"I am . . . just someone who is here."

Naturally, I was a bit taken back. What struck me most was that though I was hearing Cheryl's voice, it had a cold, taunting tone I could never have imagined coming from her—a sweet, gracious, soft-spoken woman.

"All right, who is 'I am'?" said Keith. "I command you in the name of Jesus to speak. Only the Lord God Almighty is I AM."

"I am just someone who is here," came the voice as Cheryl continued to shiver.

"Don't shiver!" Keith ordered. "I command you in name of Jesus to stop that." The shivering stopped immediately, although it returned several more times and needed continual rebuking. "Only the Lord God Almighty can say 'I AM.' Holy Spirit, release your light. Give us discernment. You have said that if we need wisdom, all we have to do is to ask you in Jesus' name. Now, I command this spirit to speak and make its presence known without physical effects. Stop the trembling in the name of Jesus. Who are you? What are you doing there?"

"Getting attention."

"How?"

"The shivers!"

Thus began a five-hour session of prayer unlike anything I had ever experienced or could have imagined. After about three hours, we paused, and I called home. My wife, Sarah, was very upset because of some uncharacteristic, out-of-control behavior on the part of one of our young children. Sarah told me that about an hour earlier he had become very sarcastic and had run out of the house and up the street. She and one of our other children had had to bring him home. This was not at all like him.

"It's like someone turned a beehive loose in our home," Sarah said. "What are you doing? Can you come home quickly?"

I talked to our son and prayed for my family over the phone, assuring them that I would be home as soon as possible.

Then I returned to Jim and Cheryl's living room. We all prayed again for our families, sealing them under the protection of Jesus Christ, and then proceeded with the deliverance. By this time, I was leading the prayer.

For reasons I couldn't understand, the demon resisted coming out until we named it correctly. It had given us several false names, which we had simply used for the time being, acting as if we accepted them as its real name.

"We command you to leave in the name of Jesus," I said. "I am getting impatient with all this argument. You must go. What is your real name? I order you to tell me in the name of Jesus."

"How did you know that wasn't my real name?"

"The Holy Spirit gives us his wisdom. You are to tell us who you are."

"Why do you need to know my name?"

"It's only right that I call you by your name. You must be proud of it."

"It makes me weak to say it. . . ."

"Tell me your name!"

Cheryl suddenly shut her eyes and pursed her lips in defiance, like a five-year-old who refuses to take her medicine. Until this point, Cheryl's eyes had been wide open, never blinking.

"Stop that!" I commanded. "Open your eyes and look at me."

"It starts with p—that's all I'm going to tell you."

We began to pray for wisdom and mentioned several words that began with p: pain, power. Then Pastor Chuck said, "Punishment. Your name is Punishment!" Cheryl's eyes flew wide open in amazement!

"Who gave you the clue?"

"The Holy Spirit revealed it to us. He wants you to

leave now, Punishment. Your time here is finished. You are very weak now."

At this point, Cheryl's husband took over and ordered the demon to leave his wife.

"Punishment, I am the head of this household, and I command you in the name of Jesus to come out of my wife. Do not hurt her. Come out now. Do not return."

Cheryl began to gasp and cough as though she were choking. She asked for a pillow. We commanded Punishment to release her and to let her breathe. We called on the Holy Spirit to fill her lungs with air and to drive the wicked spirit out. Cheryl held the pillow against her stomach so she could cough. She coughed several times and then lay back with a smile and a look of relief, her eyes blinking frequently. She had never blinked the entire time we were in dialogue with the demon!

"How do you feel?" I asked.

"I feel released," she said in a whisper.

Then a spirit—a holy spirit!—of joy and celebration fell upon us. We sang praise choruses and hymns and laughed as we spoke of the victory of Jesus. We had seen him work!

I remember driving home thinking that my life and ministry would never be the same. I had just experienced something I read about often in the New Testament. I had encountered a "being" that I had never encountered before and had seen the power of God bring visible, dramatic change in a person's behavior. While I could not deny my experience—and the witness of two other pastors and a dear married couple—I realized I had a lot of thinking and rethinking to do.

Cheryl continued to battle cancer. Although the disease had taken a toll on her body, from that time on, she had a peace and "inner quiet," as she called it, that she had never experienced before. About eighteen months later, she went to be with the Lord. Though she hadn't experienced a physical healing, we didn't view her death as a defeat because she had been healed spiritually. Cheryl, her family, and all who knew her had experienced the power and grace of God in ways that put death in perspective. As God's Word proclaims in 1 Corinthians 15:54-58:

> Death is swallowed up in victory.
> O death, where is your victory?
> O death, where is your sting?

For sin is the sting that results in death, and the law gives sin its power. How we thank God, who gives us victory over sin and death through Jesus Christ our Lord!

So, my dear brothers and sisters, be strong and steady, always enthusiastic about the Lord's work, for you know that nothing you do for the Lord is ever useless.

WHAT IS SPIRITUAL WARFARE?

I have not had any experiences nearly as vivid or dramatic since that time with Jim and Cheryl. But I have had a number of other "battles" that have convinced me of the truth of Paul's statement in Ephesians 6:10-12: "A final word: Be strong with the Lord's mighty power.

Put on all of God's armor so that you will be able to stand firm against all strategies and tricks of the Devil. For we are not fighting against people made of flesh and blood, but against the evil rulers and authorities of the unseen world, against those mighty powers of darkness who rule this world, and against wicked spirits in the heavenly realms."

The Bible tells us that there are a number of forces antagonistic both to God and to those who seek to follow God's ways. Spiritual warfare is the conflict waged by the forces of darkness against God and God's creation, especially humankind. This battle between good and evil is being fought on earth, in our personal life, and in the spiritual realms.

As we consider this battle, however, it would be a mistake to fall into dualism—the philosophy that God and the devil, as sources of good and evil, are equal but opposite forces. As will be shown, God is infinitely superior to evil and will secure the ultimate victory. Nevertheless, evil is a real, substantial foe bent on our destruction. God, working through Jesus Christ, won the decisive battle at the Cross. Evil continues in this world until Christ returns and finally implements his victory (see I Corinthians 15:24-28). While God will win in the end, we, at the present time, are part of the "mop-up operations."

Spiritual warfare is much broader than conflict with evil beings. Evil in every form aims to defy the Lord and destroy God's creation. In a later chapter, we will see that there are three primary enemies: the world, the flesh (our rebellious, sinful nature), and the devil. All three seek to compromise our allegiance to God and to prevent our obedience to God's will. In this book, we will discuss the spiritual resources and weapons that are available to us as we battle against temptation, distraction, and deception.

Before we start taking a look at our enemies and the weapons we can use to fight them, you may have some basic questions about the whole topic of spiritual warfare. For example, many people ask the following:

WHAT IF I FIND IT HARD TO BELIEVE IN THE DEVIL AND DEMONS?

For some—perhaps even most of us—this will be "weird stuff." Don't think I don't know that! I still find myself feeling resistant and skeptical on a regular basis. But I have made a commitment to study God's Word objectively and to be open to whatever God will do. Are you ready to make that commitment? Or will you set limits on what's real and possible? Only you can answer that question.

Personally, I have found many people to be very receptive to these matters. Some have even admitted to having had experiences similar to mine but were reluctant to tell anyone. The strong interest in Frank Peretti's ground-breaking novels on spiritual warfare, *This Present Darkness* and *Piercing the Darkness,* are an intriguing testimony. But you don't need to be convinced of the reality of spiritual warfare in order to keep reading this book. I appreciate a principle I first heard stated by Dr. David Hubbard, the late president of Fuller Theological Seminary: "We must give everybody room to pass." Total agreement is not necessary in order to maintain respect and fellowship.

My purpose in writing this book is not to coerce faith or to convince you of the existence of demons. I respect you, the reader, too much to do that. My goal is to illustrate, through the study of God's Word and the testimony of credible witnesses, the possibility—indeed the reality—of a dimension of spiritual life that you may not have fully considered. Why? To empower faithfulness to God and resistance to temptation.

I have been cautioned by some about the dangers of overemphasizing this subject. While I agree that there is a danger, I believe there is also a danger in ignoring the subject of spiritual opposition. I think, for example, of the importance of both health clubs and hospitals. Health clubs are useful because they help us get fit and avoid disease, while hospitals are necessary to treat illnesses and injuries. Like those who go to a health club, we should give our primary attention to achieving and maintaining spiritual health. At the same time, however, we need to be informed and well armed in case of spiritual attack.

I find that more and more people like me, who have grown up in traditional Christian settings, are being confronted with spiritual realities that they can't explain apart from genuine spiritual opposition. It may be that the Lord is calling us to new dimensions of spiritual activity, to be stretched, to be intentional in the broadening of our ministry. If so, we must develop keener spiritual sensitivities so that we can discern and overcome evil in its various forms—in order that God's will can be done *on earth as it is in heaven.*

WHAT ARE THE BENEFITS OF
UNDERSTANDING SPIRITUAL WARFARE?

Before going into detail about the nature of evil and about strategies for victory, I want to address the concern of some that the study of evil may make us more vulnerable to its power and influence. Quite the opposite is true.

When we really understand the power and presence of evil, we gain a much deeper appreciation for the practical benefits of what God has done through Jesus Christ. We take so much for granted because we understand so little about the way things really are. John summarizes the reason for Jesus' coming to earth, saying, "But the Son of God came to destroy these works of the Devil" (1 John 3:8). Jesus' victory has a much broader impact than releasing individuals from the consequences of sin. He has, in fact, transformed the entire cosmic order. "For God in all his fullness was pleased to live in Christ, and by him God reconciled *everything* to himself. He made peace with *everything in heaven and on earth* by means of his blood on the cross" (Colossians 1:19-20, emphasis added). Nothing will ultimately withstand Christ's triumph.

When we understand the enemy, we are less vulnerable to intimidation. And Jesus' victory brings us his power: "He who is in you is greater than he who is in the world" (1 John 4:4, RSV). Memorize this verse and remind yourself of this truth daily. The seeds of intimidation sprout in the soil of ignorance. We allow ourselves to be bullied by evil. Understanding, however, exposes the limitations of evil. We are freed from the deceptions and illusions that may weaken our resolve.

Awareness of the influence and strategies of evil also enables us to better help others. As we are able to discern and confront all our problems, including demonic obstacles and sources of resistance, we have a more biblically sophisticated framework for diagnosing evil and a greater repertoire of responses to confront it.

What's more, taking spiritual warfare seriously deepens the intensity of our commitment to our own sanctification and discipleship. When we become aware of evil's pervasive influence, we realize that our thoughts, words, actions, and wounds can be entry points for the evil one. We are more eager to guard against temptation and to seek the Lord's protection.

I invite you to explore this subject with an open mind and willingness to test what you read by the Word of God. I ask you to consider your own response to the questions I was forced to grapple with:

- How can I believe in demonic beings in this age of scientific enlightenment?
- Didn't this sort of thing stop with the New Testament?
- Aren't there more simple and "realistic" psychological and physiological explanations for spiritual phenomena?

All these questions lead to one even more basic question: What is your view of spiritual reality? We'll explore that question in the next chapter.

CHAPTER TWO

Seeing the World through Different Eyes

My friend Jerry was telling me about some experiences he and his wife, Leslie, had had during a period when she was struggling with depression. One night while they were talking and praying, the Lord "invaded Leslie's heart," to use Jerry's words. Leslie felt a fresh touch from Jesus, a nearness she hadn't felt in some time. The next morning she read the Bible for several hours. Her hunger for God's Word led her to devour it at every opportunity. Several weeks later, however, depression closed back in. This time it came quickly and forcefully. Leslie had just come home from shopping when she felt the cold, all-too-familiar darkness descend. She began crying, went into the bathroom to get tissues, and looked into the mirror. As she did, she felt an overwhelming revulsion arise within her. She looked herself straight in the eye and almost snarled. Then she heard a voice very different from her own speak through her own lips, saying, "I hate you! I hate you!"

Leslie was shocked and nearly panicked by the whole

experience. "I didn't know what to do," she told me later. "In desperation I cried out, 'In the name of Jesus Christ, be gone!'" A few moments passed, and then she felt a peace settling on her. "It was like the sun peeking through the darkest clouds after a thunderstorm. I could still see the darkness and feel the effects, but it was getting lighter." Since that incident, Leslie says, although she sometimes has "blue days," she has never again been overwhelmed with darkness.

I want to stress that, from my point of view, Jerry and Leslie are ordinary folks. In fact, they told me that, while they believed the Bible, they had never thought there was any truth to present-day accounts of experiences with demons or demonization. But they were forced to rethink what they believed because of a personal experience they couldn't explain. "The most surprising thing," Jerry told me, "was that Leslie's experience was actually consistent with the Gospels! But we found we hadn't really paid attention to that part of the Bible." Leslie's experience jolted them into looking at their world in a different way.

WHAT SPIRITUAL MAP ARE YOU USING?

Your map of the world in many ways determines your experience of life. Likewise, a new map can unleash incredible change. This was demonstrated vividly by the birth of the modern world following the voyages of navigators such as Magellan and Columbus. By the time these great explorers came along, medieval Europe had been severely depressed. The population of most nations had been decimated by the black plague, which in some cities in the mid-1300s was killing hundreds of people daily. Besides the plague, the Europeans were cut off from trade with the East by the Muslims, who held Asia Minor and controlled most of the northern and eastern Mediterranean coastline. Life was stagnant, and there seemed to be no hope of change.

One of the major areas of stagnation was in geography. Europeans were still using the map of Ptolemy (a Greek philosopher who lived in the second century A.D.), which ended at the equator. At the borders of the map, cartographers drew dragons to indicate the unknown. In all but a few courageous souls, these dragons instilled fear and the resistance to exploration.

Then a cluster of individuals arose who refused to accept the prevailing map and worldview.

Portuguese-born Spanish explorer and navigator Ferdinand Magellan, who lived in the late 1400s and early 1500s, was the leader of the first expedition to sail completely around the world. Magellan set out to reach the East Indies by sailing westward from Europe, which no one was sure could be done. Although he died en route, his companions completed the voyage.

Then there was Christopher Columbus (1451–1506), an Italian-Spanish navigator who sailed west across the Atlantic Ocean in search of a route to Asia. Instead of finding Asia, he landed in the Caribbean and was credited with discovering North America.

Columbus and Magellan—along with other worldview challengers like Nicolaus Copernicus (1473–1543), whose sun-centered view of the solar system would eventually replace the prevailing view that the earth was the center of the universe—proved that the worldview that had dominated Europe for over fifteen hundred years was wrong! Within a decade or two of the discoveries of Columbus, Magellan, and Copernicus, an explosion of change was set in motion throughout Europe. The Protestant Reformation, which had been simmering for nearly a century, suddenly burst into bloom. Inventions, such as the development of the printing press, the watch, and the telescope, multiplied exponentially. The Renaissance was born with its proliferation in the arts and literature. People rediscovered the intellectual vitality of the ancient Greeks and were treated to the creativity of Shakespeare and other literary artists. Europe experienced the brilliance of the Enlightenment after centuries in the Dark Ages.

It would seem that the worldview of the ancient and medieval periods had blocked people from seeking new solutions. New discoveries resulted in a new worldview, generating incredible energy and change.

WHAT IS A WORLDVIEW ANYWAY?

A worldview is "that complex set of patterns in terms of which people think and behave."[1] It is like your map of reality. Chuck Colson writes, "[Our worldview] is simply the sum total of our beliefs about the world, the 'big picture' that directs our daily decisions and actions. . . . Every worldview can be analyzed by the way it answers three basic questions: Where did we come from, and who are we *(creation)*? What has gone wrong with the world *(fall)*? And what can we do to fix it *(redemption)*?"[2]

While we may not be conscious of the fact, we all have a worldview that determines how we see life and how we behave. We must ask ourselves, "What is my worldview? What limits and boundaries have I accepted? Are there dragons I have not dared to challenge?" Some may hear these questions as an invitation to an "anything goes" philosophy—but wait just a minute before you put the book down! My real question is this: Does your worldview, your spiritual map, reflect the landscape of life presented in the Bible?

THE WORLDVIEWS OF TODAY

Many of us operate on the basis of assumptions that have arisen from Western (European and North American) thought and philosophy. As we embark on the twenty-first century, we live in a culture dominated primarily by a scientific, rationalistic approach to life. This worldview is based on a mechanistic view of the universe as a closed system with fixed and inevitable laws. Dr. Charles Kraft, professor of anthropology and intercultural communication at Fuller Theological Seminary, describes five specific characteristics of this view of life.[3]

First, this worldview is naturalistic. When someone gets sick, our first question concerns what caused the illness. We assume a naturalistic agent, such as a germ. In contrast, most non-Western peoples ask a supernatural question: Which spirit caused the illness, or who has been offended?

Second, this worldview is materialistic. We focus far more on objects than on relationships, defining success in purely material terms. In contrast, many non-Western cultures define prosperity in terms of family members, relatives, and community relationships.

Third, it is humanistic. We believe man is the measure of all things and has nearly unlimited potential for accomplishment. In contrast, other cultures acknowledge the central role of God/gods in the direction of life.

Fourth, it is rationalistic—governed primarily by reason. We explain all things in terms of logic and reason, and we subject "non-objective" experience to the same criteria used for science. In contrast, other cultures interpret life in a way that includes intuition and emotion, allowing room for mystery and for realities beyond what we can perceive through our senses.

Finally, it is individualistic. We value independence, assuming that we are solely responsible for our life and that taking other people into account is "optional" as we choose to include them. In contrast, other cultures have a sense of corporateness, believing that the behavior of one person may bring blessing or punishment on the whole group.

At the heart of the modern Western worldview is an antisupernatural assumption that God doesn't exist—or that God is not actively involved in daily life. This worldview presumes that supernatural forces are fabrications. They are seen as expressions of myth, as primitive expressions that have been surpassed in our scientific understanding. There are many who demythologize the teaching of the Bible. For example, they interpret *principalities and powers* (see Romans 8 and Ephesians 6) as speaking exclusively of human government and political systems. As we will see, this is a biased interpretation of the text, neglecting the explicit intentions of the biblical authors. Those with this worldview don't expect to see miracles or confrontations with evil beings. That is where the dragons live.

A BIBLICAL WORLDVIEW

When I had my first experience of observing what appeared to be demon involvement—and then heard other stories, such as the one opening this chapter—I really struggled with my assumptions. I turned to people I could trust for counsel and direction. One of those was Dr. Paul Pierson, then dean of the School of World Mission at Fuller Theological Seminary in Pasadena, California. Paul admitted that he too had struggled with these subjects but was greatly helped when he heard the consistent witness of credible believers from other cultures around the world.

Paul had heard, for example, of a situation in which a group of Christian believers were passing out gospel tracts in an African village, but the villagers refused to accept the tracts. Then, when the team met those very same people on the other side of the street, they gladly accepted the literature. Paul said that the group then learned that a witch doctor lived on the first block, and he had put a curse against Christians who "trespassed" on his turf. The villagers actually weren't aware of the curse, nor of their own antagonistic behavior toward the missionaries when they were on the cursed block.

As one missiologist, Dr. Paul Hiebert, tried to explain occurrences of supernatural signs and wonders on the mission field, he came up with the concept of the "Excluded Middle."[4]

Hiebert explained that most Westerners have a two-tiered model of reality. In this model, the lower tier is the empirical world of our senses and ordinary experience from which the supernatural is excluded. The second tier comprises the transcendent world beyond ours, including heaven and hell, angels and demons. This realm of religion and faith doesn't impinge on our daily experience.

Hiebert asserts, however, that a biblical worldview has three tiers. Between the lower and upper levels is a middle level that includes the spiritual forces *on this earth* (my emphasis). These spiritual forces interact with the world and humanity in daily life. They include angels, demons, and other supernatural forces. The evil forces enter human lives through such practices as witchcraft and sorcery—while on the side of good are the power and gifts of the Holy Spirit working for God. Obviously, if this is true, it means we must take much more into account than most of us are accustomed to doing. This is not easy for most of us.

BEWARE THE LURE OF FASCINATION

As we consider the validity of spiritual warfare in our day, we must not only establish a biblical worldview, we must also guard against two basic errors: First we must avoid undue fascination with the subject. Human beings have always been intrigued by the "dark side" of life, imagining monsters and supernatural horrors. We have also been attracted to paranormal phenomena and are tempted to dabble in practices that seem to promise us power and control over our destinies. This unhealthy interest lies behind God's warning in Deuteronomy 18:10-14 against witchcraft and sorcery:

> And do not let your people practice fortune-telling or sorcery, or allow them to interpret omens, or engage in witchcraft, or cast spells, or function as mediums or psychics, or call forth the spirits of the dead. Anyone who does these things is an object of horror and disgust to the Lord. It is because the other nations have done these things that the Lord your God will drive them out ahead of you. You must be blameless before the Lord your God. The people you are about to displace consult with sorcerers and fortune-tellers, but the Lord your God forbids you to do such things.

When we start to consider seriously the existence and practices of evil beings, we can be sidetracked into psychic practices or into trying to map out the landscape of hell or into figuring out the hierarchy of Satan's demonic organization. We can be distracted by charts and formulas for overcoming evil charms and spells. All this must be consistently, earnestly resisted.

We must take our cue from the Bible. Very little description is given of the kingdom of evil. Why? Because we are to follow Paul's counsel in Colossians 3:1-4:

> Since you have been raised to new life with Christ, set your sights on the realities of heaven, where

Christ sits at God's right hand in the place of honor and power. Let heaven fill your thoughts. Do not think only about things down here on earth. For you died when Christ died, and your real life is hidden with Christ in God. And when Christ, who is your real life, is revealed to the whole world, you will share in all his glory.

This does not mean we are to ignore every subject about life here on earth or about the powers of evil. But it does mean that we shouldn't delve deeply where the Bible speaks little. We should also follow Jesus' ways. Jesus was remarkably simple and direct in his confrontations with evil. He simply took authority over evil and moved on. He explained the ways of the kingdom of God without giving undue attention to the enemy. Having said this, however, we would benefit from a clear understanding of our evil opponents. Just who are our enemies? We'll find out in the next chapter.

NOTES

1. Charles Kraft, *Christianity with Power* (Ann Arbor, Mich.: Vine Books, 1989), 54.

2. Charles Colson and Nancy Pearcey, *How Now Shall We Live?* (Wheaton, Ill.: Tyndale House Publishers, Inc., 1999), 14.

3. Kraft, *Christianity With Power*, 58.

4. This material is derived from Paul Hiebert, "The Flaw of the Excluded Middle," *Missiology: An International Review*, 10, no. 1 (January 1982): 35–47, quoted in John Wimber, *Power Evangelism*, (San Francisco: Harper San Francisco, 1986), 76–81.

CHAPTER THREE

Meet the Enemies

Around 400 B.C. the brilliant Chinese war strategist Sun Tzu wrote, "Know the enemy and know yourself and in one hundred battles you will never be in peril. When you are ignorant of the enemy but know yourself, your chances of winning or losing are equal. If ignorant both of your enemy and of yourself, you are certain in every battle to be in peril."[1]

Nowhere is this truer than in matters of our faith. The Christian faith and experience cannot be understood apart from the reality that we are engaged in a mortal battle with the enemies of God. Most people seem to think of Christianity as a moral system or code of ethics. In reality, the moral code is just one dimension of a much broader design. That design is nothing less than the reestablishment of God's reign and rule on this rebel earth. The Lord's Prayer contains a very clear statement of our purpose as followers of Jesus: "Thy kingdom come. Thy will be done in earth, as it is in heaven" (Matthew 6:10, KJV). What does this mean?

The people of God are to begin a visible establishment of the rule of God on earth. We catch glimpses of this in Acts 2 and 4, where new believers demonstrate a selfless fellowship in community and work to bring the effects of salvation to every aspect of life.

We are living in a rebellious world, subject to sin and the curse of God's judgment. "If the world hates you, keep in mind that it hated me first. If you belonged to the world, it would love you as its own. As it is, you do not belong to the world, but I have chosen you out of the world. That is why the world hates you" (John 15:18-19, NIV).

Followers of Jesus Christ form "a rebel colony," living *in* the world without being *of* the world (see John 17:16). An analogy from history may help us understand our role. From 1936–1939, Francisco Franco led an uprising against the Spanish republic in Madrid. Franco's General Mola, who was besieging Madrid with four columns of soldiers from the outside, boasted that he had a "fifth column" within the city that was secretly aiding his forces. Since then, the concept of a "fifth column" has come to represent any group that aids the enemy from within its own country.

In a sense, believers in Jesus Christ form a fifth column in the world. We are living in a world that has been, for the time being, subjected to the curse and to the power of evil. We are not only sojourners and pilgrims (see Hebrews 11) on this earth but also agents of God sent to break the strongholds of evil and reclaim this world and all within it for his glory. As such, we participate in bringing the kingdom of God on earth.

Our failure to grasp the central image of the kingdom has led to a fragmented faith and an immature discipleship. It has limited our vision and goal. As much as we may not like the image, God is at war against the kingdom of darkness, against those forces of evil that seek to deface and destroy his creation. Let's look more closely at the kingdom of darkness.

Followers of Jesus actually face a threefold enemy: the world, the flesh, and the devil. All three conspire against us—sometimes individually, sometimes in concert.

OUR ENEMY: THE WORLD

The world is spoken of in two senses in the Bible. The first use of the term *world* is simply to designate the physical creation (see Psalm 89:11; Psalm 90:2; Matthew 25:34). In this use of the word, the world is valuable and to be managed with wise stewardship. But the term world also refers to the realm under the control of Satan. This world is evil, a snare to our spiritual lives (see Romans 12:2 and I Corinthians 1:20-28). We are faced here with one of those "both-and" truths of our faith. The world is both good and evil, depending on the particular issue at stake. As the old hymn says, "This is my Father's world," yet there is a sense in which this world is under the rule of Satan. Satan's "authority" is acknowledged when Jesus says, "I will not speak with you much longer, for *the prince of this world* is coming. He has no hold on me" (John 14:30, NIV, emphasis added).

God is Creator and still the ultimate ruler, but human

disobedience (see Genesis 3) brought death into the world and somehow gave Satan authority.

The world ruled by Satan is a primary rival for our affections and attention. As John warns us in his first letter:

> Stop loving this evil world and all that it offers you, for when you love the world, you show that you do not have the love of the Father in you. For the world offers only the lust for physical pleasure, the lust for everything we see, and pride in our possessions. These are not from the Father. They are from this evil world. And this world is fading away, along with everything it craves. But if you do the will of God, you will live forever. (1 John 2:15-17)

Other translations, such as the RSV, describe the temptations of the world as "the lust of the flesh and the lust of the eyes and the pride of life" (1 John 2:16). We will discuss the flesh more specifically later in this chapter. What we want to note here is that this unholy trinity—the lust of the flesh, the lust of the eyes, and the pride of life—distracts our attention and diverts our efforts from the things of God. We are tempted to become self-seeking, absorbed by the offers of worldly pleasures, prestige, and possessions.

The world mimics and opposes God the Father, our Creator. The primary sin with respect to the world is idolatry. Whether our idols are literal objects of worship, such as the images of false gods of other religions, or "secular" idols of money, material things, or spiritual practices forbidden by Scripture (see Deuteronomy 18:9-14), they tempt us away from worshiping and serving the only true God.

How do we resist the temptations of the world? Primarily by rejecting the lie that these things have lasting value. The material things of life are simply tools that we are to use in God's service. Material things such as food, clothing, money, homes, and modes of transportation all have their place, but they must never take God's place in our life.

The book of Ecclesiastes offers a sound, sober assessment of life in this world:

> I said to myself, "Come now, let's give pleasure a try. Let's look for the 'good things' in life." But I found that this, too, was meaningless. "It is silly to be laughing all the time," I said. "What good does it do to seek only pleasure?" After much thought, I decided to cheer myself with wine. While still seeking wisdom, I clutched at foolishness. In this way, I hoped to experience the only happiness most people find during their brief life in this world.
>
> I also tried to find meaning by building huge homes for myself and by planting beautiful vineyards. I made gardens and parks, filling them with all kinds of fruit trees. I built reservoirs to collect the water to irrigate my many flourishing groves. I bought slaves, both men and women, and others were born into my household. I also

owned great herds and flocks, more than any of
the kings who lived in Jerusalem before me. I
collected great sums of silver and gold, the
treasure of many kings and provinces. I hired
wonderful singers, both men and women, and
had many beautiful concubines. I had everything
a man could desire!

So I became greater than any of the kings who
ruled in Jerusalem before me. And with it all, I
remained clear-eyed so that I could evaluate all
these things. Anything I wanted, I took. I did not
restrain myself from any joy. I even found great
pleasure in hard work, an additional reward for
all my labors. But as I looked at everything I had
worked so hard to accomplish, it was all so
meaningless. It was like chasing the wind. There
was nothing really worthwhile anywhere.
(Ecclesiastes 2:1-11)

The writer, usually thought to be King Solomon,
concludes:

Here is my final conclusion: Fear God and obey
his commands, for this is the duty of every
person. God will judge us for everything we do,
including every secret thing, whether good or
bad. (Ecclesiastes 12:13-14)

The world promises far more than it can ever deliver.
It competes for our attention but, like fool's gold, it is all
glitter and of no value. Jesus' followers learn to use and

enjoy the appropriate blessings of the world without clutching them too closely. They are aware from the stories of Demas (see 2 Timothy 4:10) and Ananias and Sapphira (see Acts 5) that the love of the world can compromise and even destroy the most committed believers.

OUR ENEMY: THE FLESH

In Scripture, the term *the flesh* refers not simply to our physical nature, but to the rebellious human nature—the impulses and willfulness that are set in direct opposition to God (see Romans 7:5, 18, noting that the literal term flesh, which is in the KJV, is translated as "sinful nature" or "old sinful nature" in many contemporary translations such as the NLT and the NIV). The flesh is our sinful nature in its broadest sense. It mimics and opposes the Holy Spirit within us. That is why an essential aspect of spiritual warfare is knowing not only the enemies outside ourself but also knowing ourself. We need to be continually assessing our weaknesses and our vulnerabilities. This helps us guard against temptation and attack. As part of the assessment process, we should consider questions such as:

- What do I find most attractive in the world?
- What interferes most with my spiritual life and progress?
- If the devil were to attack me, where would he most likely hit?

The primary avenue to our flesh is temptation, which attracts and attacks through our senses, our desires, and our selfish ego. The flesh within us meets temptations that often come through the world. As James writes, "And remember, no one who wants to do wrong should ever say, 'God is tempting me.' God is never tempted to do wrong, and he never tempts anyone else either. Temptation comes from the lure of our own evil desires. These evil desires lead to evil actions, and evil actions lead to death" (James 1:13-15).

We find ourselves at war within ourselves. We are constantly challenged to put off the flesh and put on the way of Christ (see Colossians 3). Indeed, the process of sanctification—growing into the likeness of Christ—is primarily a process of overcoming our fleshly nature through the power of the Holy Spirit within us. (Specific strategies for battling temptation will be presented in chapter 7.)

Although fleshly temptations can be our downfall, it is possible to turn them to good effect. Thomas Brooks wrote:

> Temptation is God's school wherein he teaches his people to see a greater evil in sin than ever, and a greater emptiness in the creature than ever, and a greater need of Christ and free grace than ever; a school wherein God will teach his people that all temptations are but his goldsmiths, but which he will try and refine, and make his people more bright and glorious.[2]

OUR ENEMY: THE DEVIL AND DEMONS

Evil is not simply an impersonal, random occurrence in this world. Nor does it simply arise from within us. The

Bible clearly depicts evil as having a personality and a measure of structure and organization. In Colossians 1:13 we read, "For he has rescued us from the one who rules in the kingdom of darkness, and he has brought us into the Kingdom of his dear Son." In John 12:31, Jesus speaks of his coming death and resurrection as the judgment and overthrow of Satan: "The time of judgment for the world has come, when the prince of this world will be cast out."

A variety of Scriptures indicate the broad power and prerogative of the evil one and his hosts. Daniel 10:13 tells how an answer to prayer was delayed by demonic interference. In 1 Chronicles 21:1 we read about Satan's inciting of King David to take a census. In the book of Job, Satan is given almost unlimited power to harm Job and his family. In the temptations of Jesus, the devil exerts remarkable power, even offering the Son of God all the kingdoms of the world. What is interesting is that Jesus does not contradict the legitimacy of Satan's claim over the worldly kingdoms. Consistent with Jesus' later teaching in John, he tacitly acknowledges Satan's role.

Several phrases in Scripture indicate the rule of evil. *Principalities and powers* (see Romans 8:38; Ephesians 1:21; 3:10; 6:12; and Colossians 1:16; 2:10; 2:15) is a phrase that usually refers to demons or fallen angels who, along with Satan, hold positions of authority. Some demythologize these terms to mean social, economic, and political systems, but that is a function of a Western worldview.

What seems very clear is that Satan and one-third of the angelic beings fell from heaven and have laid claim to this world. (See Revelation 12:3-4; the "stars" referenced in this passage are usually interpreted to be the angels that fell from heaven and became demons.) Their rule has been progressively challenged by God, culminating in direct confrontation in the incarnation, death, resurrection, and ascension of Jesus. After rejecting Satan's attempt to assert his power and influence from the beginning, Jesus launched a full-scale attack against the kingdom of darkness through preaching, teaching, and healing. The conflict between the two kingdoms was especially clear when he cast out demons.

MORE ABOUT THE DEVIL

The evil one goes by a number of names and descriptions in the Bible. He is called "Satan," which means "adversary." We see him in this role in Job 1:6-12, when he accused Job of loving God solely because God had blessed him with so much. Satan also played the role of adversary in Zechariah 3:1 when he stood at the right hand of Joshua the high priest "to accuse him." He is also called the "accuser of our brethren" in Revelation 12:10 (RSV).

The evil one is called:

- The *devil* (Matthew 4:1), a term which, like *Satan,* has in its background the concept of an accuser who brings a complaint against someone
- *Beelzebub* (Matthew 10:25 and 12:24), a term which literally means "lord of the flies," referring in a derogatory way to his leadership over the demons

- A *murderer* (John 8:44)
- A *liar* and the *father of lies* (John 8:44)
- The *ruler of this world* (John 14:30)
- The *god of this world* (2 Corinthians 4:4)
- *Abaddon,* a Hebrew term, and *Apollyon,* a Greek term, names used in Revelation 9:11 for destroyer, describing the locustlike destruction Satan and his hosts bring on earth

Two Old Testament passages are often interpreted as giving additional background and history on Satan. The first is Isaiah 14, which describes the fall of the king of Babylon. Many see this passage as working on two levels. It seems to apply to the historical level, but the being described in verses 12-14 seems to be larger than life. The name Lucifer, which is often used for Satan, comes from this passage and may lay behind Paul's reference to Satan's being able to counterfeit himself like an angel of light (2 Corinthians 11:14).

Ezekiel 28 is a similar passage in which a prophecy is given against the king of Tyre, the capital of Phoenicia, just north of Israel. Like the prophecy in Isaiah, this passage speaks against a dominant characteristic of pride on the part of one who seeks to rival God, a theme that causes some commentators to see links to Satan. Whether or not these interpretations are correct, they do portray the judgment of God against the proud—and the ultimate prideful being is Satan.

There are a number of other terms used in connection with Satan, but the point should be clear that the evil one is a significant opponent, not to be taken lightly.

Understanding that, we also need to remember that Satan is a creature, created by God. He shares *none* of the divine attributes of being all-powerful (omnipotent), ever present everywhere (omnipresent), or all-knowing (omniscient). We are often careless in our speech, attributing characteristics to the evil one that belong only to God. The Bible, however, portrays Satan's limitations. He can only act within the limits that God permits (see Job 1:12; 2:6; 1 Corinthians 10:13). Satan may even be used to advance God's causes (see 2 Corinthians 12:7). As we will see, God has given us ample promises and power to overcome the evil one. We can rejoice in Paul's confident statement that "the God of peace will soon crush Satan under your feet" (Romans 16:20, RSV).

MORE ABOUT DEMONS

When Jesus began his ministry, he taught with authority and stirred up the opposition. In Mark 1:21-28 we read about Jesus' first confrontation with a demon:

> Jesus and his companions went to the town of Capernaum, and every Sabbath day he went into the synagogue and taught the people. They were amazed at his teaching, for he taught as one who had real authority—quite unlike the teachers of religious law.
>
> A man possessed by an evil spirit was in the synagogue, and he began shouting, "Why are you bothering us, Jesus of Nazareth? Have you come

to destroy us? I know who you are—the Holy One sent from God!"

Jesus cut him short. "Be silent! Come out of the man." At that, the evil spirit screamed and threw the man into a convulsion, but then he left him.

Amazement gripped the audience, and they began to discuss what had happened. "What sort of new teaching is this?" they asked excitedly. "It has such authority! Even evil spirits obey his orders!" The news of what he had done spread quickly through that entire area of Galilee.

Jesus rebuked the demon, who recognized the ultimate significance of Jesus' appearance—to destroy them (see I John 3:8).

How do we, at the beginning of the third millennium, interpret the true nature of demons? Many Western commentators discount and dismiss the possibility of supernatural beings and treat them as "superstitious" designations for psychological disturbance. But we must face the fact that Jesus treated them as independent entities with individual personalities. If Satan is a specific personality, so are demons.

Demons are evil spirits, the fallen angels that serve Satan. They can disrupt human life in a number of ways. The Bible says that demons cause certain maladies such as deafness (Mark 9:25), blindness (Matthew 12:22), dumbness (that is, the inability to speak; Luke 11:14), and mental disorders (see Luke 8:27). It must be noted that there are far more typical or natural causes for these maladies; there is no biblical reason to conclude that these conditions are usually caused by demons.

What is the significance of Jesus' conflict with demons? Luke 10:17-20, in which Jesus refers to the disciples' effectiveness at healing and casting out demons, gives us a clue:

> When the seventy-two disciples returned, they joyfully reported to him, "Lord, even the demons obey us when we use your name!"
>
> "Yes," he told them, "I saw Satan falling from heaven as a flash of lightning! And I have given you authority over all the power of the enemy, and you can walk among snakes and scorpions and crush them. Nothing will injure you. But don't rejoice just because evil spirits obey you; rejoice because your names are registered as citizens of heaven."

One commentator says that "the casting out of the devils proves the victory over the devil gained by Jesus and thus the breakthrough by the kingdom of heaven. . . . The great moment of the breaking down of Satan's rule has come and at the same time that of the coming of the kingdom of heaven. The redemption is no longer only future but has become present. In this struggle it is Jesus himself who has broken Satan's power and who continues to do so."[3]

Jesus' miracles, including exorcism, were the visible fulfillment of God's promises, making visible the coming of salvation.

So how do we combat the enemy? Before we consider the weapons of spiritual warfare, we need to consider who we are in Christ. Ultimately, victory lies more in who we are than in what we do.

NOTES

1. Sun Tzu, *The Art of War,* trans. and intro. by Samuel B. Griffith (Oxford: Oxford University Press, 1963), 84.

2. Thomas Brooks, *Precious Remedies Against Satan's Devices* (London: The Banner of Truth Trust, 1968), 178.

3. Herman Ridderbos, *The Coming of the Kingdom* (Philadephia: The Presbyterian and Reformed Publishing Company, 1962), 62–64.

CHAPTER FOUR

Where Victory Begins

Victory in spiritual warfare begins long before we take the field of battle. Some military leaders say that victory begins at basic training camp when a raw recruit is physically conditioned, mentally toughened, and trained in the principles of war. But others would assert that there is another even more important element: being on the right side! For followers of Christ, victory begins with being on God's side—which gives us our identity.

UNDERSTANDING OUR IDENTITY AS CITIZENS OF THE KINGDOM OF GOD

We have already studied the nature of the kingdom of darkness, learning much about our three enemies: the world, the flesh, and the devil. But knowing the enemy is only half the equation for victory. The other half is understanding our own identity and resources as children of God, empowered by the Holy Spirit.

The apostle Paul roots our hope in the fact that our

salvation has caused us to emigrate to a new kingdom. He tells the Colossian believers:

> We also pray that you will be strengthened with his glorious power so that you will have all the patience and endurance you need. May you be filled with joy, always thanking the Father, who has enabled you to share the inheritance that belongs to God's holy people, who live in the light. For he has rescued us from the one who rules in the kingdom of darkness, and he has brought us into the Kingdom of his dear Son. (Colossians 1:11-13)

Paul expresses the same idea in Philippians. "But whatever happens to me, you must live in a manner worthy of the Good News about Christ, as citizens of heaven" (Philippians 1:27). As citizens of heaven, we have not only a new standard for living, but also an enduring reason to hope.

> Dear brothers and sisters, pattern your lives after mine, and learn from those who follow our example. For I have told you often before, and I say it again with tears in my eyes, that there are many whose conduct shows they are really enemies of the cross of Christ. Their future is eternal destruction. Their god is their appetite, they brag about shameful things, and all they think about is this life here on earth. But we are citizens of heaven, where the Lord Jesus Christ

lives. And we are eagerly waiting for him to return as our Savior. He will take these weak mortal bodies of ours and change them into glorious bodies like his own, using the same mighty power that he will use to conquer everything, everywhere. (Philippians 3:17-21)

As citizens of God's kingdom, we have rights and privileges, responsibilities and duties. But above all, we have the assurance that we live under the protection of the King of all Creation. We have the assurance of his ultimate victory. The powerful promise is that the day will come when "the whole world [will] become the Kingdom of our Lord and of his Christ, and he will reign forever and ever" (Revelation 11:15).

One day, the battle will be over, the fighting will cease, and the mighty Lamb and Lion of God will present the kingdom in victory to the Father. Paul describes this process in 1 Corinthians 15 when he writes about the change that has come through Jesus' resurrection:

Everyone dies because all of us are related to Adam, the first man. But all who are related to Christ, the other man, will be given new life. But there is an order to this resurrection: Christ was raised first; then when Christ comes back, all his people will be raised.

After that the end will come, when he will turn the Kingdom over to God the Father, having put down all enemies of every kind. For Christ must reign until he humbles all his enemies beneath his feet. And the last enemy to be destroyed is death. For the Scriptures say, "God has given him authority over all things." (Of course, when it says "authority over all things," it does not include God himself, who gave Christ his authority.) Then, when he has conquered all things, the Son will present himself to God, so that God, who gave his Son authority over all things, will be utterly supreme over everything everywhere. (I Corinthians 15:22-28)

We must never lose sight of these promise-prophecies. They fuel our spiritual stamina, lighting the way in the dark nights of trial and temptation. We know the end of the story! We may not understand how it will unfold step by step, but we cling to the hope, indeed the certainty, that we are on the winning team.

REMEMBERING WHO WE ARE

The evil ones most often begin their attack at the point of our identity and self-confidence. When we lose sight of our identity as citizens of God's kingdom, we become most vulnerable. This is a difficult concept to grasp, but it becomes clear when we see it illustrated. In their Gold Medallion Award–winning books, *Tales of the Kingdom* and *Tales of the Resistance*, Karen and David Mains tell the story of an orphan boy who had been scarred on his face during the evil practice of branding in the Enchanted City. The Enchanted City is a realm that has fallen under the spell of an evil sorcerer known both as the Enchanter and also as the fire wizard. Eventually Scarboy, as the boy was called, escapes the Enchanted City and enters the Great Park, a place of goodness and healing. In that place he is adopted and given a new name, Hero.

The time comes for him to return to the Enchanted City to join with the forces of the Good King in overthrowing the wicked Enchanter. In the scene described below, Hero has just witnessed the first encounter of the Good King, who had come in the guise of a humble person, with the evil Enchanter. The Good King had been severely blasted by the fire wizard but was unbeaten. He had warned the fire wizard that the time of wicked enchantment was coming to an end. We pick up the story when the Good King had left along with the crowds.

> Suddenly he [Hero] knew he was standing alone in the presence of the Enchanter in the bone cold night air. He quickly covered his cheek [where he had been branded] with his hand, pulled his collar up around his neck, and started to creep away.
>
> "Scarboy!"
>
> Too late.
>
> "Scarboy!"
>
> Hero stopped. He waited for a cudgel blow to the head, a burning poker in his back. He expected the death drums to paralyze his soul, the song of the Naysayers to strike terror in his heart—but the strange silence continued, except for the old name, spoken by the old enemy.

But instead of giving into his old fears, Hero began to remember his new identity.

Then he heard it. The sound rose unbidden from some distant place, the one-note sound of the Rite of Adoption; flutelike, faint, faraway. *H-m-m-m-m-m-m-m-m*, it began. One lonely sound.

"SCARBOY!" the Enchanter shrieked, calling the old name frantically, as though he sensed power diminishing.

Little time; soon the silence would be broken. The one-note hum swelled, filling his heart, beating wildly beneath his breastbone, gladdening his ear.

That was it! He might be scarred, but he was Scarboy no longer. He didn't belong here, in this evil place, this city doomed by enchantment. His home was Great Park, the King's palace. His people were the people of Great Park—Mercie and Caretaker were his true parents.

Hero began to walk. Without looking back, without yielding himself to the eyes of the wizard who called his name, he walked to the beat of the hymn in his own heart. He no longer belonged here. The power of evil over him *was* diminished.[1]

THE DANGER OF THE WRONG FOCUS

The story of Scarboy illustrates the fact that *evil gains power when we focus on our wounds and failings, but it loses power when we focus on our new name and our redeemed nature*. In a sense, evil in all its forms has only the power we allow it to have over us.

This principle is explained more fully in my book *Questions God Asks, Questions Satan Asks*. In a discussion of the wilderness temptations of Jesus, we see that during those temptations, Satan had limited power over Jesus. When Satan took Jesus to the high place in Matthew 4:6 (NIV), he said, "If you are the Son of God, . . . throw yourself down." What was Satan doing? He was trying to persuade Jesus to act. What's interesting is that Satan couldn't just push Jesus off the pinnacle! All he could do was coax Jesus to do it himself. Just as Satan's power over Jesus was limited, so his power over us is limited.

You and I need to understand the limits of Satan's power. The devil can try to persuade, but he cannot compel. He can try to tempt you to do something, but he can't force you to do it. He can hold out drugs, but he can't put them in your veins or make you swallow them. He can hold out lustful temptation, but he can't make you get involved in it. He can hold out a bribe, but he can't make you take it. He may set the stage, but we are the actors.

The devil's only means of success is to get us to say yes—to provoke our willing participation, making us fully responsible. He can take us to the highest places, but he cannot make us leap.[2]

Let me say it again: *Evil gains power when we focus on our wounds and failings, but evil loses power when we focus on our new name and our redeemed nature.* When our focus shifts from evil to the truth of God, we break the enchantment of wickedness. While the evil one would have us be self-absorbed and fearful, God's Word calls us to remember who we are in Christ. What, then, is our identity?

FOCUSING ON OUR NEW IDENTITY

Victory begins when we live moment by moment in the power of our adoption in Christ. As Paul writes, "So you should not be like cowering, fearful slaves. You should behave instead like God's very own children, adopted into his family—calling him 'Father, dear Father.' For his Holy Spirit speaks to us deep in our hearts and tells us that we are God's children. And since we are his children, we will share his treasures—for everything God gives to his Son, Christ, is ours, too" (Romans 8:15-17).

A prince wouldn't stoop to common thievery, because he already has the most prized possessions of the kingdom. Likewise, we will not succumb to temptation or intimidation when we hold in our hearts the treasures of our salvation.

Since Satan is a "liar and the father of lies" (John 8:44), we need to be on constant guard against falsehood and deception, especially when it comes to our self-understanding. We must tell ourselves the truth about who we are and resist acting contrary to our identity in Christ. The Bible gives us a number of affirmations concerning our identity and value in Christ. A brief survey of the Scriptures reveals that:

- We are the salt of the earth (Matthew 5:13)
- We are the light of the world (Matthew 5:14)
- We are joint heirs with Christ Jesus (Romans 8:17, KJV)
- We are subjects of God's special care (1 Peter 5:6-7)
- We are children of God (1 John 3:1)

We could continue to list phrases, but these alone should encourage us, giving us a firm anchor in the storms of temptation and spiritual warfare. But there is yet one more reason for hope and security. Not only are we citizens of the heavenly kingdom—indeed members of God's family—we are also indwelt by the living God, the person of the Holy Spirit. As Paul says, we are the temple of the Holy Spirit (1 Corinthians 6:19).

REMEMBERING WHO LIVES WITHIN US

There is no greater encouragement than the fact that "the Spirit who lives in you is greater than the spirit who lives in the world" (1 John 4:4). The Holy Spirit brings the power of God into our daily life. The power of God which was active in Creation and in the mighty acts of God in the Old Testament has now been given to the believer. To fully understand this, we must take a moment to review the work of the Spirit.

Rather than being a vague concept, the Holy Spirit is truly a divine person of the Trinity, expressing the power of God in creation. We see this when we remember that the Hebrew and Greek words for "spirit," "breath," and "wind" are the same. The Spirit was active in the creation of the world (see Genesis 1:2) and in imparting life to human beings (see Genesis 2:7). We see the work of the Spirit in the mighty wind that turned back the flood (Genesis 8:1) and parted the waters in the Exodus (Exodus 14).

Michael Green calls the Holy Spirit a "violent, invading force" (see Isaiah 40:7). "In speaking of the

'Spirit of the Lord,' " he writes, "the Old Testament writers significantly retain this emphasis on God's violent invasion from outside our experience, disturbing and mysterious like the wind. It is their way of stressing that the Beyond has come into our midst, and we can neither organize nor domesticate him."[3]

The Spirit has empowered and equipped God's people for service (see Exodus 31:1-5), inspired the prophets (see 2 Samuel 23:2), and produced moral character and living (see Psalm 51 and Psalm 139:7, 23-24). In the Old Testament, the Spirit came upon people, but did not reside within them (see Numbers 11:29). Yet the promise was given that the Spirit would eventually take up residence within God's people (see Jeremiah 31:31-34; Ezekiel 36:24-27; and Joel 2:28-29).

Jesus promised the Spirit would be given to his followers (see Luke 11:13 and John 14:16-17). That promise was fulfilled following his resurrection when the Holy Spirit came upon all who believe (see Acts 2).

The power of God within us enables to do spiritual battle in a number of ways. First, as the Holy Spirit nurtures the "fruit of the Spirit" in our life, we begin standing against evil. The Spirit battles the flesh, the old human nature, by shaping Christlike character in God's people. Paul describes this process in his letter to the Galatians:

> When you follow the desires of your sinful
> nature, your lives will produce these evil results:
> sexual immorality, impure thoughts, eagerness
> for lustful pleasure, idolatry, participation in

demonic activities, hostility, quarreling, jealousy, outbursts of anger, selfish ambition, divisions, the feeling that everyone is wrong except those in your own little group, envy, drunkenness, wild parties, and other kinds of sin. Let me tell you again, as I have before, that anyone living that sort of life will not inherit the Kingdom of God.

But when the Holy Spirit controls our lives, he will produce this kind of fruit in us: love, joy, peace, patience, kindness, goodness, faithfulness, gentleness, and self-control. Here there is no conflict with the law.

Those who belong to Christ Jesus have nailed the passions and desires of their sinful nature to his cross and crucified them there. If we are living now by the Holy Spirit, let us follow the Holy Spirit's leading in every part of our lives. (Galatians 5:19-25)

Second, the Spirit equips God's people for ministry by giving us his gifts and spiritual power that can be used in part to overcome evil (see Acts 5:1-11 for the story of Ananias and Sapphira; Acts 5:16; and 1 Corinthians 12:7). Jesus inaugurated the age of the Spirit, making a fuller experience of God possible for us. This includes a continuing process of being transformed into Christlikeness by the Spirit at work within us.

Victory can be ours because we are on the right team, because of our redemptive relationship with the Lord, and because we have the resources of the Holy Spirit. But how do we use these truths in the battle? By fighting with spiritual weapons. We'll learn more about these in the next chapter.

NOTES

1. David and Karen Mains, *Tales of the Resistance* (Elgin, Ill.: Chariot Books, David C. Cook Publishers, 1986), 37–41.

2. Douglas J. Rumford, *Questions God Asks, Questions Satan Asks* (Wheaton, Ill.: Tyndale House Publishers, Inc., 1998), 145.

3. Michael Green, *I Believe in the Holy Spirit* (Grand Rapids: Wm. B. Eerdmans Publishing Company, 1975), 19.

CHAPTER FIVE

Know Your Weapons

It's important that we choose the right weapons—both offensive weapons and defensive weapons—when engaging in spiritual battle. Unfortunately, we humans have a tendency to rely on our own resources instead of God's power and protection, a fact we see illustrated in the account of David and Goliath in 1 Samuel 17. Reading this story, we see that when David offered to go to battle against Goliath, Saul insisted David wear Saul's armor.

> David put it on, strapped the sword over it, and took a step or two to see what it was like, for he had never worn such things before. "I can't go in these," he protested. "I'm not used to them." So he took them off again. He picked up five smooth stones from a stream and put them in his shepherd's bag. Then, armed only with his shepherd's staff and sling, he started across to fight Goliath. (1 Samuel 17:39-40)

Although Saul wanted to rely on man-made armor, David proclaimed his full confidence in the power of God:

> David shouted [to Goliath] in reply, "You come to me with sword, spear, and javelin, but I come to you in the name of the Lord Almighty—the God of the armies of Israel, whom you have defied. Today the Lord will conquer you, and I will kill you and cut off your head. And then I will give the dead bodies of your men to the birds and wild animals, and the whole world will know that there is a God in Israel! And everyone will know that the Lord does not need weapons to rescue his people. It is his battle, not ours. The Lord will give you to us!" (1 Samuel 17:45-47)

What are some of the worldly weapons we are tempted to use? We may look to human alliances, as did the Israelite kings (see God's judgment against Jehoshaphat in 2 Chronicles 20:35-37), provoking consistent rebukes from the Lord. Or we may be tempted to depend on money, or position, or prestige, which are often useless and even counterproductive in the most important struggles of life. We may try to rely on human logic, only to be ensnared in arguments. We may be tempted to take revenge or treat others as they have treated us—which usually leads to prolonged and escalated struggles.

Worldly armor will not protect us against the Goliaths of spiritual warfare. In fact, it could hinder us by preventing us from seeing the creative hand of God bringing triumph in unimagined ways. So we must rely on God's power—in other words, we must put on God's armor.

GO INTO BATTLE WEARING THE WHOLE ARMOR OF GOD

The first biblical use of the armor image is presented in Isaiah 59:15-17:

> Yes, truth is gone, and anyone who tries to live a godly life is soon attacked.
> The Lord looked and was displeased to find that there was no justice. He was amazed to see that no one intervened to help the oppressed. So he himself stepped in to save them with his mighty power and justice. He put on righteousness as his body armor and placed the helmet of salvation on his head. He clothed himself with the robes of vengeance and godly fury.

Even as the Lord wore armor to secure his victory, so he now equips us in Christ. Ephesians 6:10-18 gives a comprehensive presentation of the resources God provides to help us stand against temptation and spiritual attack. Read the passage twice and take a few moments to reflect on the various aspects of Paul's exhortation.

> A final word: Be strong with the Lord's mighty power. Put on all of God's armor so that you will be able to stand firm against all strategies and

tricks of the Devil. For we are not fighting against people made of flesh and blood, but against the evil rulers and authorities of the unseen world, against those mighty powers of darkness who rule this world, and against wicked spirits in the heavenly realms.

Use every piece of God's armor to resist the enemy in the time of evil, so that after the battle you will still be standing firm. Stand your ground, putting on the sturdy belt of truth and the body armor of God's righteousness. For shoes, put on the peace that comes from the Good News, so that you will be fully prepared. In every battle you will need faith as your shield to stop the fiery arrows aimed at you by Satan. Put on salvation as your helmet, and take the sword of the Spirit, which is the word of God. Pray at all times and on every occasion in the power of the Holy Spirit. Stay alert and be persistent in your prayers for all Christians everywhere.

As Paul reflected on spiritual battle, he undoubtedly considered the Roman soldiers he had seen. They not only looked impressive, but their armor was effective. How much more effective is the equipment God gives us.

THE BELT OF TRUTH

Wearing a belt was a sign that a Roman soldier was on active duty. The belt was used to gather the soldier's loose robe up and out of the way for swift, unhindered movement. When his belt was off, a soldier was at rest; when on, he was ready to fight.

It is essential to put on the "belt of truth" in our battle with evil, because Satan is a liar and the father of lies (John 8:44). He lays his traps through deceit and deception. We see this in his first attack against Eve in the Garden of Eden. The serpent (identified later as Satan in Revelation 12:9 and 20:2) deceived Eve, using insinuation to cause her to doubt God. Indeed, Satan's basic formula for temptation has remained the same across the ages. It usually involves five steps. (The following five steps are explained more fully in my book *Questions God Asks, Questions Satan Asks*.)

First, the tempter appeals to our reason with malicious, perverted logic, usually questioning God's word. "Did God really say . . . ?" (See Genesis 3:1).

Second, Satan uses innuendo and exaggeration. He tries to get us to resent God's law, to feel it is too restrictive. He also tends to inflate our own egos, so that we feel we are beyond God's "oppressive" regulations.

Third, Satan engages us in debate, knowing that if we enter an argument with him, we will usually lose the battle. Puritan preacher Thomas Brooks wrote of Satan's seductive logic, "It is safe to resist, it is dangerous to dispute." [1]

Fourth, the devil convinces us to deny consequences. If he can get us to think that God will overlook our sin, or that we will be easily forgiven, or that it's no big deal, then the voices of godly conscience and reason are silenced.

The fifth step is enticement. When our mind is darkened and our sinful desires are inflamed, we take the bait and embrace the temptation while the evil one slithers away.

Our first weapon, therefore, is truth—truth that refutes Satan's lies and exposes his deception. When we understand the nature of deception and can answer the arguments of evil, light drives out the darkness. Instead of allowing the deceiver any room in our heart, we take God's Word as true and trustworthy. Even when we don't fully understand God's direction or even his restrictions, we do understand that his purposes for us are based in love. Satan's purposes are grounded in hatred, malicious through and through.

Putting on the belt of truth means that we refuse to be party to lies or deceit of any kind. It means speaking the truth in love and confessing our sin when we have failed. It means that, even when we are tempted to hide, as Adam and Eve did (see Genesis 3), we acknowledge that only truth sets us free (John 8:32). Our own experience confirms that we can actually feel relieved when a hidden act becomes known. Though we may at first be embarrassed or ashamed, we know that we can stand taller on the shoulders of truth. That's why the evil one loathes it so much.

When we commit to the way of truth, the battle can often be won "without a shot being fired," as the saying goes. The lesson: Silence the first whisper of temptation with the firm voice of truth.

THE BODY ARMOR OF GOD'S RIGHTEOUSNESS

Though there are many levels of meaning in the idea of "putting on God's righteousness," the primary one is that we are in fact made righteous, forgiven, and accepted through faith in Jesus Christ alone. We don't wear our own medals on our chest; we wear his! This shields us against Satan's accusations of our guilt and unworthiness. Our confidence is in what God has already done for us in Christ Jesus through his death and resurrection. We claim nothing for ourselves. As a favorite hymn, "Rock of Ages," puts it:

> *Nothing in my hand I bring,*
> *Simply to thy cross I cling.*

A second aspect of "putting on God's righteousness" is our being conformed to the image of Christ through obedience. As we grow in faith, we learn to flee temptation, to guard against the exploitation of our weak spots, and to exercise self-control. We break free not only from sin's penalty but also from its power (see Romans 6:11-18). This is not to say, however, that we will ever reach a point in this life when we can rely on our righteousness as our primary protection. As William Gurnall writes, "Evangelical holiness [that is, holiness that comes through the gospel] makes the creature rather [more] willing than able to give full obedience. The saint's heart leaps when his legs do but creep in the way of God's commandments."[2] While we continually pursue godly living, we know that our hope lies in our faith in Christ.

THE SHOES OF THE GOSPEL OF PEACE

In Paul's time, a soldier's shoes were especially important because enemy troops would often scatter sharp rocks and fragments of pottery along roads to slow an opposing army's progress. We often take our own shoes for granted until we get blisters or other ailments—then we realize just how important shoes are. As we enter spiritual battle, our walk must be cushioned by equipment that can take the shocks and stresses of daily life. The gospel of peace should always mediate between the world and us. Whether we walk on smooth, rough, flat, hilly, wet, or desert spiritual terrain, we walk in the power of the gospel, which gives us sure footing, illumines our path, sustains our strength, and carries us to the goal.

There is another aspect to the image of shoes as part of our defensive armor. In the Scriptures, feet are used as a poetic image for a messenger. Isaiah 52:7 says, "How beautiful on the mountains are the feet of those who bring good news of peace and salvation, the news that the God of Israel reigns!" This speaks of the messenger who runs from the front lines of the battle to inform the king and the people of a victory. But Paul applies this image to the ultimate message of peace and reconciliation (see Romans 10:15). We march through life with this message. Though evil tries to silence us or to distract us, we are surefooted in taking the glorious truth, the Good News, wherever we go.

THE SHIELD OF FAITH

In Ephesians 6:16 Paul describes faith as a shield. He is referring to the large, door-shaped shield, called a *scutum* by the Romans (in contrast to the small, round *aspis* or *pelta* the Romans also used). The scutum was designed with an iron frame, with a metal boss (plate) on the front center. This metal was then covered with several layers of leather. When the shield was soaked in water before battle, the wet leather would extinguish flaming arrows, and the metal covering would prevent arrows and javelins from piercing the shield. Because the shield was large enough for a soldier to stand behind, it was able to protect his entire body.[3]

We can take cover behind the shield of faith for protection against the temptations, accusations, and persecutions the evil one aims at us. "Flaming darts" is an apt description of these attacks, which come swiftly, at unexpected times, and are aimed directly at the heart. Like King David on the rooftop, we are in danger of being ambushed by darts of lust. Shots of greed, jealousy, envy, and anger can threaten to pierce our defenses. But faith deflects them. Faith that is based solely on the Lord's power and protection can be like a force field around us. "This is the victory that has overcome the world, even our faith. Who is it that overcomes the world? Only he who believes that Jesus is the Son of God" (1 John 5:4-5, NIV). The New Living Translation puts it this way, "For every child of God defeats this evil world by trusting Christ to give the victory. And the ones who win this battle against the world are the ones who believe that Jesus is the Son of God."

Faith deflects or destroys the darts of doubt and deception. By faith, we can have the mind of Christ (see 1 Corinthians 2:16). By faith, we can claim the Lord's protection. Faith looks beyond the immediate threat to assurance of God's strength to endure. Faith looks beyond the immediate attraction of the temptation to the far horizon of God's blessing for those who resist. Psalm 91 is perhaps the most powerful expression ever written of faith in the midst of battle. This psalm so inspired courage that it was often sewn into soldiers' uniforms and printed on small cards for soldiers to carry into battle.

> He who dwells in the shelter of the Most High,
>> who abides in the shadow of the Almighty,
> will say to the Lord,
>> "My refuge and my fortress;
>> my God, in whom I trust."
> For he will deliver you from the snare of the fowler
>> and from the deadly pestilence;
> he will cover you with his pinions,
>> and under his wings you will find refuge;
>> his faithfulness is a shield and buckler.
> You will not fear the terror of the night,
>> nor the arrow that flies by day,
> nor the pestilence that stalks in darkness,
>> nor the destruction that wastes at noonday.
> A thousand may fall at your side,
>> ten thousand at your right hand;
>> but it will not come near you.
> You will only look with your eyes
>> and see the recompense of the wicked.
> Because you have made the Lord your refuge,
>> the Most High your habitation,
> no evil shall befall you,
>> no scourge come near your tent.

> *For he will give his angels charge of you*
>> *to guard you in all your ways.*
> *On their hands they will bear you up,*
>> *lest you dash your foot against a stone.*
> *You will tread on the lion and the adder,*
>> *the young lion and the serpent you will trample under foot.*
> *Because he cleaves to me in love, I will deliver him;*
>> *I will protect him, because he knows my name.*
> *When he calls to me, I will answer him;*
>> *I will be with him in trouble,*
>> *I will rescue him and honor him.*
> *With long life I will satisfy him,*
>> *and show him my salvation. (RSV)*

Rather than allowing anxiety and worry to drain away our courage, we can fuel our faith with affirmations of truth from God's Word. We hold high the shield of faith when we remind ourselves that, moment by moment, our God is watching over us, protecting us at all times.

THE HELMET OF SALVATION

In the era that Paul was writing, a soldier's helmet was a primary means of identifying his army and allegiance. The design, special insignia, and other features (such as colored plumes or feathers) indicated whose side a soldier was on. When we put on the helmet of salvation, we signal that we are on the side of salvation. Note that the word *salvation* has two primary meanings. The first has to do with healing, as in our term "salve," a name for a healing ointment. Jesus Christ has healed us from the mortal wound of sin. He has restored our spiritual health. The second meaning of the word salvation has to do with deliverance. We have been released from captivity to the enemy. When we wear the helmet of salvation, we acknowledge that we belong to the God who has made us whole again and set us free from bondage. We also announce that we are committed to fighting in order to bring that full salvation to others.

There is a second aspect to the helmet. Not only does it announce our allegiance, but, even as a physical helmet guards our head, so the helmet of salvation protects our minds and thoughts. In 1 Thessalonians 5:8-9 (NIV), Paul refers to the helmet of salvation as an expression of hope. "But since we belong to the day [as opposed to the night of dark powers and disobedience], let us be self-controlled, putting on faith and love as a breastplate, and the hope of salvation as a helmet. For God did not appoint us to suffer wrath but to receive salvation through our Lord Jesus Christ."

Such hope is essential for us because two of the devil's chief weapons against believers are discouragement and despair. The devil and his evil ones will do anything in their power to prevent salvation. Their ultimate goal is to cause us to turn our allegiance from God, joining their wicked rebellion. Poet John Milton captured their vindictive desires in these lines spoken by Beelzebub in *Paradise Lost*:

> *Seduce them to our Party, that their God*
> *may prove their foe, and with repenting hand*
> *Abolish his own works. This would surpass*

> *Common revenge, and interrupt his joy*
> *In our confusion, our Joy upraise*
> *In his disturbance. . . .* [4]

But hope drives this threat far from us. As the psalmist proclaims,

> *Though an army besiege me,*
> *my heart will not fear;*
> *though war break out against me,*
> *even then will I be confident. (Psalm 27:3, NIV)*

THE SWORD OF THE SPIRIT

The sword described by Paul in Ephesians is the double-edged short sword of the Roman infantry called the *machaira*.[5] It was smaller than the swords of most other armies and therefore initially ridiculed by other soldiers who carried longer, more impressive weapons. But the short swords worked far better in close combat because the Romans could wield them more easily and swiftly.

We can pierce evil's defenses with the sword of the Spirit—the Word of God. This power was seen in Jesus' response to Satan's temptations in the wilderness. In response to every temptation, Jesus replied, "The Scriptures say." (See Matthew 4:4, 6, and 10.) The Word cut through the spell of lies the evil one sought to cast. As the psalmist said, "Thy word have I hid in mine heart, that I might not sin against thee" (Psalm 119:11, KJV).

The sword is our only offensive weapon. Hebrews

4:12-13 (NIV) describes it as a dynamic, animated, and animating power:

> For the word of God is living and active. Sharper than any double-edged sword, it penetrates even to dividing soul and spirit, joints and marrow; it judges the thoughts and attitudes of the heart. Nothing in all creation is hidden from God's sight. Everything is uncovered and laid bare before the eyes of him to whom we must give account.

As God's Word makes a home in our heart, the Holy Spirit uses it to guard and guide us at all times. The Holy Spirit is the power within the Word, making it effective in the work of condemnation, conviction, and conversion.

The sword of the Spirit is also our means to overcome opposition to the truth. Dorothy Sayers wrote, "It is fatal to let people suppose that Christianity is only a mode of feeling; it is vitally necessary to insist that it is first and foremost a rational explanation of the universe."[6]

As we master the Word of God, we learn the mind of God, the ways of God, and the ways of evil. We are transformed by the renewal of our mind (Romans 12:2), and the veil of deception is lifted from our heart (see 2 Corinthians 3:12-18). Meditate on God's Word day and night—and it will protect you night and day.

CHOOSE YOUR WEAPONS

In the days of duels, the challenger would give his opponent a choice of weapons. Perhaps you can recall hearing the phrase "pistols at dawn" while watching some melodramatic movie. The choice of weapons, of course, was based on what the challenged person felt would be most effective. Likewise, we must choose our spiritual weapons based on what would be most effective against a particular opponent in a particular kind of confrontation.

The first point to keep in mind when choosing a weapon for spiritual warfare is that we are to become skilled with all the weapons—both offensive weapons and defensive weapons—available to us. No soldier would go into battle without his complete armor because the pieces all worked together.

We must take the time to grow in our understanding and our ability to use each piece of spiritual armor. We need to ask ourselves questions like these:

- Is my commitment to and understanding of truth becoming a part of my thinking and my character? Is my integrity improving?
- Am I living in the full confidence of God's righteousness through Christ? Am I vulnerable to temptations because I'm relying on my own efforts? Am I growing in the obedience of faith?
- Is my faith evident to people in my daily life, wherever I am, whatever I am doing? Am I prepared to share my faith with them?
- Do I carry the shield of faith, responding with hope instead of pessimism, with confidence in God's care instead of anxiety? Are there any flaming darts coming at me that need to be extinguished right away?

- Am I wearing the helmet of salvation as a clear testimony that I belong to the Lord and am serving him in all I do?
- Am I learning to wield the Word of God with increasing skill? Do I know it so well that I can find the direction I need for all situations?

What type of spiritual battle are you facing right now? Are there strong temptations, interpersonal conflicts, or unusual difficulties that are disrupting your spiritual progress? Reexamine the pieces of God's armor. Keeping in mind that we need them all, identify the piece of armor that would be especially helpful to you at this time. Picture Christ as clothing you in the armor, and then write a prayer seeking God's grace to achieve victory.

The pieces of God's armor mentioned in Ephesians—the belt of truth, the body armor of God's righteousness, the shoes of peace, the shield of faith, the helmet of salvation, and the sword of the Spirit—are critically important weapons in our ongoing war against evil. But here's one more weapon in our arsenal. It is so powerful and so multifaceted, however, that we must devote a full chapter to it. Turn the page and join me in looking at the ultimate weapon in spiritual warfare.

NOTES

1. Thomas Brooks, *Precious Remedies Against Satan's Devices* (London: The Banner of Truth Trust, 1968), 245.

2. William Gurnall, *The Christian in Complete Armour* (London: The Banner of Truth Trust, 1964), I, 409.

3. Based on material from Markus Barth, *Ephesians* (Garden City, N.J.: Doubleday & Company, Inc., 1974), 771–73.

4. John Milton, *Paradise Lost,* in *Complete Poems and Major Prose,* ed. by Merritt Y. Hughes (New York: The Odyssey Press, the Bobbs-Merrill Co., Inc., 1957), part II, lines 368–73.

5. *Ephesians,* 771–73.

6. Dorothy Sayers, *The Whimsical Christian* (New York: MacMillan Publishing Company, 1978), 34.

CHAPTER SIX

The Ultimate Weapon—Prayer

Prayer is at the very heart of every aspect of spiritual warfare. It is the means by which we are continually armed, supplied, directed, and restored in the battle. It is our lifeline to our Heavenly Headquarters.

It is no coincidence that Paul concludes his exhortation on spiritual armor with a call to pray. "Pray at all times and on every occasion in the power of the Holy Spirit. Stay alert and be persistent in your prayers for all Christians everywhere" (Ephesians 6:18). In this simple verse, Paul gives six basic principles for warfare prayer.

PRAY ALWAYS

Prayer is the essential link between us and God. It is one of the most practical ways for us to keep our attention riveted on the Lord, instead of being overwhelmed by the enemy. In one of his sermons on the Lord's Prayer, Gregory of Nyssa (330–395) writes about the role and effect of prayer in a believer's life:

The effect of prayer is union with God, and, if someone is with God, he is separated from the enemy. Through prayer we guard our chastity, control our temper, and rid ourselves of vanity. It makes us forget injuries, overcomes envy, defeats injustice and makes amends for sin. Through prayer we obtain physical well-being, a happy home, and a strong, well-ordered society. . . . Prayer is the seal of virginity and a pledge of faithfulness in marriage. It shields the wayfarer, protects the sleeper, and gives courage to those who keep vigil. . . . It will refresh you when you are weary and comfort you when you are sorrowful. Prayer is the delight of the joyful as well as the solace of the afflicted. . . . Prayer is intimacy with God and contemplation of the invisible. . . . Prayer is the enjoyment of things present and the substance of things to come.[1]

This rich description of prayer is a long way from the trivial "give me, give me" prayers that mark most believers' lives. I used to think that prayer was coming to God to get what I wanted. Now I realize prayer is coming to God to receive what he has for me. Prayer is an oasis in the desert of life. It is the power source of spiritual vitality. Understanding this broadens our concept of prayer and makes the idea of continual prayer more understandable.

The exhortation to "pray always" is repeated several times in Scripture (see Luke 18:1; 1 Thessalonians 5:17). What seems so difficult is actually commanded; therefore, it must be possible. Prayer is to be our first response, not a last resort. Too often, however, we rely on every other possible solution before turning to prayer. Once we have exhausted all human options, we finally turn to God. We must train ourselves to pray first, to pray earnestly, to pray continually. While some try to explain this away, as if *always* didn't mean always, I am convinced that Jesus and Paul meant pray always! Granted, our prayer intensity will vary depending on the circumstances, but we can develop a much more continual conversation with God than we ever thought possible.

How can you build prayer into your daily activities? This is far easier than it sounds. Start by praying when you get up in the morning, saying simply, "This is the day the Lord has made, I *will* rejoice and be glad in it." Pray as you get dressed, asking the Lord to clothe you with the whole armor of God. Pray over your meals. Pray as you travel to school, work, or other activities— asking the Lord to help you be a faithful steward and witness to your faith. Pray as you relate to others, asking the Lord to direct your actions and conversation. Pray when you play, giving thanks to God for the refreshment of recreation. Practicing prayer in this way weaves a golden thread through every day, week, and year. In time, you will become aware that you are praying when you had made no conscious decision to do so.

This kind of continual prayer is like a holy disinfectant, keeping spiritual viruses and infections at bay. They do not disappear altogether, but they are greatly reduced in an atmosphere that is bathed in believing prayer.

USE ALL KINDS OF PRAYER

Many of us have a prejudice against certain types of prayers. Those who are more informal tend to think that written, liturgical prayers are wooden and inauthentic. But these prayers often express a depth of wisdom, insight, and theological grounding that encourages and inspires great faith. On the other hand, those who are more formal tend to minimize the value of spontaneous prayers. But these prayers often express the passion and heartfelt concerns of the intercessor.

We are to develop an ever-increasing repertoire of prayer. The Psalms give us a multitude of models. There are prayers for protection (Psalm 91), prayers of complaint in times of distress (Psalm 42), prayers against vicious enemies (Psalm 26), prayers of longing for God's nearness (Psalm 139), prayers of confession (Psalm 51), and prayers of praise and worship (Psalm 103).

An exciting exercise you might want to try is reading through the Psalms and translating them into your own experience. Other sources of inspiration for prayer are hymnbooks and books of worship, such as *The Book of Common Prayer*. These can offer ideas to enrich your prayers and broaden your concept of who God is and what he can do.

Sometimes circumstances will determine the mode and length of the prayers you use. There may be times when you can devote yourself to prayer for several hours. Other times and circumstances may be better suited to what some have called "arrow prayers." The book of Nehemiah demonstrates both types of prayer.

In chapter 1, Nehemiah is deeply moved by the destruction of Jerusalem and offers a long, intense prayer to the Lord for its restoration. Then, in chapter 2, the king whom Nehemiah serves notices his depression and asks Nehemiah what he wants. Nehemiah replies, "Then I prayed to the God of heaven, and I answered the king" (Nehemiah 2:4-5, NIV). In nearly the same moment, he prays to God and speaks to the earthly king. That's an example of an arrow prayer. I imagine him taking a deep breath and saying, "Here goes, God. Bless what I say!" What's important to remember is that Nehemiah was more prepared for the moment because he had taken time to pray beforehand.

PRAY IN THE SPIRIT

This is a rich phrase suggestive of keeping us open to the fresh wind of God's Spirit. Romans 8:26 gives us one insight into the Spirit's intercession:

> And the Holy Spirit helps us in our distress. For we don't even know what we should pray for, nor how we should pray. But the Holy Spirit prays for us with groanings that cannot be expressed in words. And the Father who knows all hearts knows what the Spirit is saying, for the Spirit pleads for us believers in harmony with God's own will.

What does this mean for us? It means that we don't have to know exactly how to pray or what words to use in order to come to the Lord. Sometimes we are intimidated or confused by the complex issues. What should we ask for? How should we pray? I would suggest that we simply come before the Lord and lay our requests before him—describing the situation without prescribing the answer. Taking a problem to the Lord—and then just being still—can bring a sense of relief and release.

There are those who think the term *praying in the Spirit* refers to supernatural influence in our prayers. They interpret it as an exhortation to use a prayer language, a type of personal "praying in tongues," in which the Holy Spirit prays through a person without that person's conscious understanding of his intercession. Others think it refers to spontaneous knowledge that comes from God, regarding a situation. Genuine followers of Jesus disagree about these things. This much we know: We must always pray in ways that honor God and respect other people.

BE ALERT

Beware of the "Gethsemane Syndrome"—the temptation to fall asleep when we are supposed to be watchful. I'm reminded of Jesus' exhortation to the disciples in Gethsemane, "Watch and pray that you may not enter into temptation" (Matthew 26:41, RSV). Puritan preacher John Owen gave several specific directions for "watching." According to Owen, a person must first watch his heart. He must pay attention to his spirit, weaknesses, corruptions, and those areas where Satan could easily get the advantage. As Proverbs 4:23 (NIV) says, "Above all else, guard [or keep watch over] your heart, for it is the wellspring of life." Second, says Owen, a person should watch his circumstances for all occasions which are "apt to entangle [his] natural temper, or provoke his corruptions." Third, the Christian should supply his heart with a rich provision of God's love and truth. To "keep the heart full of a sense of the love of God in Christ: This is the greatest preservative against the power of temptation in the world."[2]

BE PERSISTENT

It isn't enough to pray once and forget it. A number of factors can lie behind a delayed answer to prayer. (See my book *What about Unanswered Prayer?* for a thorough treatment of the possible reasons for delayed answers to prayer.) Our responsibility is clear: Pray until something happens.

Persistence sharpens our prayer sensitivities. As we continually lift particular concerns to the Lord, we often gain new insights into deeper dimensions of what is happening.

Persistence is learning to live on God's time schedule. Many of us have a short attention span. We are victims of what I call the "Quick Answer or Quit Trying" syndrome. We may attack a request with vigor and gusto, expecting quick, measurable results. If we start seeing answers, we apply continued effort to resolving the problem. But if we fail to see results, our energy and interest often decline. Soon, we may stop praying altogether or move on to other interests.

What have you given up praying about? Why? Is God calling you to begin again with a commitment to persistence? One time, while studying the parable of the persistent widow in Luke 18:1-8, I had an imaginary dialogue with the widow. (For more description and instruction on this kind of meditation, see my book *SoulShaping*.) Let me share this spiritual exercise with you because it hit at the heart of my spiritual laziness.

> Doug: *Why did the judge refuse you?*
>
> Widow: *Look at me—I am an old woman. What favor could he gain? He chose cases that served his own ends.*
>
> Doug: *How could you keep going after being rejected time after time?*
>
> Widow: *This wasn't a matter of convenience for me. Without justice I could not survive. I was not asking for riches, ease, comfort, or optional things. Only for justice—only to receive what was due me.*
>
> Doug: *Why do I find it so hard to persist like you did?*
>
> Widow: *Because you value too little and too lightly. You have so much that your true desires run shallow. You want—you get. You lose—you replace. When you realize how eternally important these spiritual matters are, you will pursue them with relentless determination. Until then, your prayer will just be a hobby.*

Prayer cannot be a hobby, an optional activity in a believer's life. As we comprehend that eternal lives are at stake, as we realize the impossibility of changing a human heart apart from the power of God, as we understand evil's defiance and defamation of God's glory, as we become more aware of our need—then we will give ourselves to more persistent prayer.

BE COMPREHENSIVE

The breadth and depth of our prayers should be constantly increasing. Most of us begin with a small circle of concern. We pray for ourselves, our family members, and a few friends. This is a good beginning, but we are called to a much wider reach in prayer. This will be a gradual process, but it must be intentional.

Paul exhorts us to pray for all believers. I have noticed that a number of congregations now include in their bulletins prayer requests for other local congregations, along with requests for their missionaries. Such practices help us to lift our eyes from our own rather small world to the larger picture of the coming kingdom of God. We can also learn who the believers are in our schools, workplaces, and community activities so that we can pray for them on a regular basis. Then our prayer can reach into all areas of life: government, business, law enforcement, education, medicine, recreation, entertainment—and the list goes on and on!

It's also important to pray for nonbelievers. The practice of making a list of nonbelievers so we can pray for them keeps evangelism on our heart and releases the power of the Spirit to work in their lives.

We need not pray for all of these all the time, but we can develop a cycle of prayer that carries us through a week or month.

A MODEL FOR PRAYER MINISTRY

Using the weapon of prayer has two dimensions. One has to do with personal prayer—prayer that is usually done in private and may be focused on ourself and our family. The other dimension of prayer is intercession. Intercession is prayer on behalf of—and often in the presence of—another person. We will never feel more spiritually alive than when we are ministering the life of Christ to another! Prayer releases the power of the gospel. God breaks the strongholds of evil, sin, falsehood, and deception through a spiritual encounter of truth and power through prayer. I have seen God work in wonderful ways through ordinary people when they simply made themselves available to pray for and with others. Praying for others in their presence can be intimidating, however, so in the following paragraphs I have offered a pattern to follow when reaching out to others through prayer ministry. This is meant to be a pattern for a broad prayer ministry, not simply for spiritual warfare. It can be used for general intercession or when praying for physical healing or emotional healing. (For purposes of simplicity, I have used the example of prayer for healing.)

Note that, while intercessory prayer ministry can take place anywhere and anytime, there are certain settings and situations that are especially appropriate. I like to invite people to come forward for intercessory prayer at the end of a worship service. Then, too, I often pray for and with people during counseling sessions or during a visit to a person's home. What is most important is that the person feel comfortable with the time and the setting.

As we move through the steps involved in prayer ministry, remember that we cannot reduce the Holy Spirit to a formula, as if prayer were a chemistry experiment. We are always to be open to the Spirit's leading. He is very creative! Still, it helps to have some guidelines. Consider this pattern, realizing that you can adapt it to your theology and "personal style."

INVITE THE HOLY SPIRIT TO LEAD
THE TIME OF PRAYER

God alone can fulfill the desires of the person who has asked for help. The Holy Spirit is the giver of all gifts and knowledge necessary for the work of intercessory prayer. We begin, therefore, by coming humbly to God in worship and confession. We ask God to have his way in this time and to bring glory to his name. We also remind ourselves to accept the authority he has given us as channels of his grace (Hebrews 4:16) and request his protection during this time of prayer.

A sample prayer would be:

> Lord, we are so thankful that we can come to you to find victory over all that opposes you and oppresses us. As we enter this time of prayer, we acknowledge that apart from you we can do nothing (see John 15:5), but that we can do all things in Christ who strengthens us (see Philippians 4:13). Now we ask you to lead us in this prayer time. Give us the gifts and the power necessary to fulfill your will. Dress us in the full armor of God. Lead us not into temptation and times of testing, but

deliver us from evil. And we will give you the praise and glory.
Amen.

BLESS THE PERSON

When a person asks for prayer, he or she often struggles with feelings of embarrassment, shame, and fear of rejection. We need to begin our time of prayer with the assurance of love and respect to help the person relax and be open to the grace of the Lord. No matter what happens—or doesn't happen—as a result of prayer, the very experience can be one of grace and affirmation.

Remember, when we pray for fellow believers, we are praying for children of God, beloved princes or princesses of his holy kingdom. Jesus Christ died for them. There is nothing about them that makes the Father love them less. We are not called to be their judge. We are to make God's grace visible to them. As people make themselves vulnerable with their requests, bless them with good words. Encourage them, for example, with what the Scripture has to say about the fruit of the Spirit (Galatians 5:22-23), about the peace that passes all understanding (Philippians 4:7), and with any blessing you sense God leading you to give. Prayers of blessing involve both words of blessing directed to the prayed-for person and requests that God will give his blessing to that person.

A sample prayer of blessing would be:

> *[Name], the Lord loves you. By faith in Jesus Christ, you are*
> *his child. He died for you and wants you to know the full*
> *freedom that he purchased for you in Christ. May the Lord*

*bless you with his love, joy, and peace. May he free you to
become all he died for you to be in Christ. I bless you with
courage for this time and ears to hear the truth of God and a
heart to accept it.*

INTERVIEW THE PERSON TO ASSESS HIS OR HER NEEDS AND DESIRES

Jesus asked the blind man, "What do you want me to do
for you?" (Mark 10:51). This may have seemed like a ri-
diculous question, when the need seemed so obvious.
But Jesus models at least three essential principles for
us. First, we are to develop a relationship with a person
in need, not simply fix their problem. Fear is one of
the enemy's chief weapons, but love is the antidote to
fear (see 1 John 4:18). So we are to take time to develop
a relationship, letting the prayed-for person know we
value him or her. This takes energy and focus, but it is
well worth the effort. Among other things, it helps develop trust and openness for the process to proceed.

There is a second principle embedded in Jesus' question. When he asked the blind man, "What do you want
me to do for you?" he was saying, in effect, that the man
had to own his problem and express his willingness to
have Jesus deal with it. So the second principle is this:
The prayed-for person must be involved in the prayer
process. The individual's will and agreement are essential. This is central to healing and deliverance.

The third principle is a bit more subtle, but it is especially important for us: We need to ask what it is that
the other person wants us to pray about. While we may
assume that we know what they need, we should not let

our assumptions direct the process. Jesus may have discerned the blind man's true heart request, but it was important for the man to make that request aloud. When we take time to ask people what it is they need, we may be surprised by how they respond. I remember a time when a man came forward for prayer. I knew he had just recently lost his job, so I thought that employment would be the subject of our prayers. But concern over his job was secondary. "I want to you to pray that God helps me renew my commitment to my marriage and my family," he said. "I think I may have lost my job so I wouldn't lose my family."

You may notice that in this model you will go back and forth between conversation with God and dialogue with the other person. Many have found this to be the most natural and effective way to conduct a prayer ministry. It allows you to "check in" with the person being prayed for and also makes the experience more natural and less formal.

In keeping with Jesus' example, after the initial prayers, ask the person his or her request. One caution here: Guard against getting too much information, such as an extended medical history or a detailed account of a story of conflict or abuse. What's important is focusing on God's touch in a person's life, not on the harm he or she may have suffered. You can begin by asking some questions such as:

"Where does it hurt?"

"When did this problem first come to your attention?"

"What was going on in your life then?"

This need not be a long process. It all depends on the nature of the issue.

MAKE A TENTATIVE ASSESSMENT AND CHOOSE A PRAYER APPROACH

As you listen to the other person, you are also listening to the Lord. You are opening yourself to God's help in discerning root causes, which can be quite challenging to comprehend. You are looking for clues to help you understand whether the person's problem is rooted in physical disease or emotional wounds—or whether spiritual warfare is involved. Spiritual warfare may be involved if the person reveals a history of overpowering temptation, occult practices, or the signs of demonic interference (we'll address these more fully in the next two chapters).

As you discern the nature of the problem, you are also asking yourself, "What kind of prayer is needed to help this person?" In trying to understand the best way to pray, you are really trying to discern what God wants to do in this person's life. We discussed different types of prayers earlier in this chapter. Here are a few more specific examples:

- You may pray for the Lord to touch this person's life and relieve his suffering.
- You may pray to break the power of a curse that seems to have plagued her life.
- You may pray to have him renounce evil and/or occult practices he has been involved with.

- You may pray with her to confess sin and repent of wrong practices.
- You may have him pronounce forgiveness to someone who has hurt him.
- You may command the powers of evil to leave the person, taking authority over evil forces in the name of Jesus.

Your primary role is to give voice to the person's need, calling upon God's mercy and grace. You may also pray through particular phrases, verses, or passages of Scripture.

ENTER INTO A TIME OF PRAYER DIALOGUE

The best way to begin this prayer time is to say, "Let's see what God will do." The goal is to encourage faith, without over-promising what God will do. We want to awaken expectation, but in humble honesty. Some attempt to bind God through a "name-it-and-claim-it" formula. I personally have seen far too many people wounded rather than helped through such practices.

The first step in this time of prayer dialogue usually consists of laying hands on the person. This is especially important when praying for healing. Touch seems to be a significant channel of healing power. It may also include anointing them with oil (see James 5:14). If you are praying for healing and the problem is "intimate," you may ask the person to put his or her hand over or near the affected part of the body and then place your hand on theirs. It is best, when possible, to have a spouse or another member of the same sex actually touch the person.

The person being prayed for should close his or her eyes while the one guiding the prayer keeps his or her eyes open to observe expressions on the person's face, manifestations of the Spirit's presence, or clues that others who are praying have something to share.

As you pray, intermittently ask the person being prayed for what is happening. If images, words, or memories are coming to consciousness, he or she should let you know. But tell the person to be honest: if it seems as if nothing is happening, that is fine.

If the person needs prayer for deliverance, you may want to follow the prayer guidelines presented in chapter 8.

ASSESS THE RESULTS

We must be honest and walk in the light. Take time to see what God is doing. If there is some visible sign of improvement (if, for example, the prayed-for person has been trembling and then stops shaking, or if his or her feelings of anxiety or depression are partially relieved), it may be good to continue praying or to schedule another time for additional prayer. In most cases, continuing prayer is important to support a person's full improvement. Studies show, for example, that only 2 percent of all healings are immediate.

If nothing seems to be happening, it may be time for more interviewing or for another prayer strategy. This is not a time to become anxious but to turn to the Lord for direction.

PROVIDE POST-PRAYER COUNSEL, ACTION, AND SUPPORT

This step addresses the questions "What must this person do to remain healed (or delivered)?" or "What should this person do if he or she was not healed or delivered?"

Jesus' parable of the wandering spirit warns us to follow up diligently *after* prayer.

> When the unclean spirit has gone out of a man, he passes through waterless places seeking rest, but he finds none. Then he says, "I will return to my house from which I came." And when he comes he finds it empty, swept, and put in order. Then he goes and brings with him seven other spirits more evil than himself, and they enter and dwell there; and the last state of that man becomes worse than the first." (Matthew 12:43-45, RSV)

Those who are accustomed to a certain way of living need counsel on how to handle a change. They may need to be instructed in how to take authority over their symptoms, especially after "deep level" or emotional healing.

The counsel may be as simple as that of Jesus to the woman, "Go and sin no more" (John 8:11). Or it may consist of referral to a recovery support group, to more extensive counseling, or to reading a portion of the Bible or a relevant book. The important thing is to realize that warfare prayer may be simply the beginning of a person's full release and restoration.

OVERCOMING THE OBSTACLES TO PRAYER

We resist this level of prayer ministry for a number of reasons. Do any of these strike a chord in you?

First, we may resist it because we fear we won't succeed. Many of us feel such a need for success that we won't risk failure. This is especially true in something as nebulous as prayer ministry. But we need to remind ourself that this is God's work. In prayer ministry, we are simply acting in obedience to his command to pray for one another. We are being loving and faithful—and leaving the results to the Lord. No matter what happens, the person will at least be blessed by the touch of someone who cares in the name of Jesus.

Second, we may resist this kind of prayer ministry because we've seen others abuse it. Nowhere has there been more abuse of prayer than in this whole area of healing and spiritual warfare. Consequently, we may be afraid of being identified with "weirdos" or charlatans who have exploited vulnerable people. But, when you stop and think about it, the answer is not to do nothing—but to provide a positive model. We can't allow the misuse of prayer to prevent the appropriate use of prayer. Such "virtue" denies the love and grace of God.

Third, we may resist because we fear others may not accept what we are doing. We may worry that the church or people we value will reject us. Such concern can be addressed in part by giving biblical reasons for our actions, taking time to lay a groundwork of education, and by developing relationships of trust. But ultimately we must address the most basic question: Who am I called to please? As Paul exhorts, "Whatever your task, *work heartily, as serving the Lord and not men,* knowing that from the Lord you will receive the inheritance as your reward; you are serving the Lord Christ" (Colossians 3:23-24, RSV, emphasis added). We have to ask ourself if our actions proceed from Scripture, faith, and the integrity of our own journey with Christ. If the answer is affirmative, then we can do no other and still be true to Christ!

Fourth, we may resist prayer ministry because we're embarrassed. This may be an understandable reason for resistance, but it is unacceptable to the Lord. "If a person is ashamed of me and my message in these adulterous and sinful days, I, the Son of Man, will be ashamed of that person when I return in the glory of my Father with the holy angels" (Mark 8:38).

Fifth, we may resist because we don't feel worthy. But a careful study of Scripture reveals that worthiness has never been a criterion when God chooses people to serve him. Consider the lives of Noah, Abraham, Isaac, Jacob, Joseph, Moses, David, Peter, and Paul. If God waited for someone worthy to come along, he'd never get anything done! God is looking for people willing to be used in spite of their unworthiness, not people who feel worthy.

Prayer, then, is the ultimate weapon in spiritual warfare. It is the foundation for all the other strategies we use to combat the world, the flesh, and the devil. We'll learn more about those strategies in the following chapters.

NOTES

1. Quoted by William Barclay, *The Daily Study Bible: The Letter to the Romans* (Philadelphia: The Westminster Press, 1957), 7.

2. John Owen, *Of Temptation: The Nature and Power of It*, ed. by Thomas Russell (London: J. F. Dove, 1823), VII, 486–88.

CHAPTER SEVEN

Battling Temptation

Late one evening, Steve lingered after a church committee meeting. He was usually one of the first out the door, but this time he hung around until everyone else was gone. He asked if I had time to talk to him privately. I could see he was deeply troubled. A business executive, he was normally even-tempered. But tonight he was obviously rattled.

"There's a woman at my office . . . ," he began and then started to shake so much that he halted in his speech, his eyes filling with tears. "There's a beautiful woman at my office who seems to be after me."

If you knew Steve, you'd know that this statement was probably not the result of an overactive imagination or ego. He was a young, trim, handsome Ivy League graduate with a vibrant personality who was extremely successful in the world of finance.

Just a year earlier, Steve and his wife, Jenny, had prayed with me in their living room to commit their lives to Christ. They'd made a commitment to put faith at the center of their marriage and home. They had one child; another was on the way. Steve seemed to be moving forward in his faith.

As he told me his story that evening, it sounded like a modern-day version of the Genesis account of Joseph and Potiphar's wife. "We've done some business deals together," Steve continued, "traveled together on a few trips, and had lunch together a few times. I knew she was recently divorced, but nothing romantic ever happened or came up. I'll admit that I was flirtatious with her, in a playful way. But everybody does that kind of stuff, don't they? She's really sharp, and I really enjoyed being with her."

He stopped, took a deep breath, and continued. "But she's started leaving little cards and notes on my desk. She's followed me in her car. And then today, she left an envelope on my desk with the map to her place and a key!

"I'm trying to resist this—I know it's wrong. But," and here he choked, unable to speak for a few moments, "before coming here tonight, I drove past her house! I would never want to do anything to hurt my wife or our children. . . . What am I going to do?"

Steve was facing a very dangerous battle of spiritual warfare. It was a classic battle of the flesh. Sexual temptation ambushes many happily married men and women. It is a common lure of the flesh, but there are many other temptations that can be just as strong and just as destructive: cheating, lying, stealing, gossip, and slander, just to name a few.

Many of us have the mistaken notion that walking

with Christ should automatically reduce the likelihood we'll be tempted. That's like expecting a sailor to experience smoother sailing by leaving a lake to sail on the ocean. When we commit our life to Christ, we enter the arena of spiritual warfare—and the battlefield is our own soul. We are thrust into the ocean of life with all its heavy seas and tempestuous storms. We must learn to navigate the rough waters that *will* come.

Whether the temptation arises from within or from outside sources, there are biblical principles that will help to lead us out of temptation. In this chapter, we'll focus on Steve's battle with sexual temptation, showing how these same principles apply for other temptations as well.

Steve and I spent several hours together, late into the evening, studying Scripture, talking, and praying. In studying Scripture, we saw that God has given us six primary lines of attack and resistance to battle temptation: seeing the lie, turning to God's truth, taking every thought captive, fleeing danger and avoiding traps, praying, and committing to fellowship and accountability. Let's look at these more closely.

SEE THE LIE

Temptation always begins with a lie. Our first line of resistance against temptation is recognizing the lie. The stirring of the flesh often happens so quickly that we barely process it on a conscious level. But when we stop and reflect, we often see the lie.

In Steve's case, the lie was that he should be able to

have great pleasure in a sexual encounter with a woman other than his wife. Additional lies accompanied the primary lie: that he wouldn't get caught, that it would be all right because they were two consenting adults, and so on and so on. Such lies ignite natural human desires, creating a fire that will consume us if not quickly snuffed out.

Lies ambush us in all aspects of life. The lie of greed, for example, says that we can be fully satisfied by money, that more money means more happiness. Yet we have story after story of wealthy people who are miserable and stories of people living in poverty who are joyful beyond expression. We must see the lie. Money does not provide lasting security—it can be lost or stolen and does no good whatsoever on judgment day (see Matthew 6:19-21). In fact, the love of money can lead us into more and more evil (see 1 Timothy 6:9-10).

Here are some other examples of common temptations, the lies behind them, and the biblical response:

Stealing. The lie may be: "They don't deserve it as much as I do," or, "They won't really miss it." The biblical response begins with the eighth commandment, "Thou shalt not steal" (Exodus 20:15, KJV). Then there's the story of Ananias's and Sapphira's attempt to deceive the Holy Spirit, as related in Acts 5. And the apostle Paul gives us these words, "I have learned how to get along happily whether I have much or little. I know how to live on almost nothing or with everything. I have learned the secret of living in every situation, whether it is with a full stomach or empty, with plenty or little. For

I can do everything with the help of Christ who gives me the strength I need" (Philippians 4:11-13).

Cheating. The lie that deceives someone who cheats in school may be: "I don't need to know this stuff for what I want to do in a career. I just need to get through this class." The biblical response points to a need for personal integrity, such as that encouraged by Paul in Colossians 4. (Note that when Paul was writing this letter, the term *slave* did not carry the racist, oppressive meaning that it does in our day. As we read this, we can properly substitute our particular life roles, such as student or employee, in place of slave.)

> You slaves must obey your earthly masters in everything you do. Try to please them all the time, not just when they are watching you. Obey them willingly because of your reverent fear of the Lord. Work hard and cheerfully at whatever you do, as though you were working for the Lord rather than for people. Remember that the Lord will give you an inheritance as your reward, and the Master you are serving is Christ. But if you do what is wrong, you will be paid back for the wrong you have done. For God has no favorites who can get away with evil. (Colossians 3:22-25)

Lying. The lie behind a lie may be: "It's no big deal. Everybody else does it!" The biblical response begins with the simple truth that the commonplace does not define morality. We can't determine what is right and wrong based on a popularity poll. Lying *is* a big deal because it attacks the very essence of a relationship: trust. When trust is gone, the foundations of a relationship are gone. But some would counter, "If I told the truth, it would ruin my relationship with so-and-so." This rationalization is usually accompanied with the justification: "It would hurt the other person too much to tell them the truth." But Jesus teaches that "the truth shall set you free" (see John 8:32). By definition, freedom cannot come through falsehood. The truth, though hard, is always better than a lie.

Substance abuse. The lie may be: "I need a break from the stress. It's a harmless way to escape." The truth is that substance abuse leads to slavery, not escape. We can find relief and lasting refreshment in the Lord alone. That's why he gave us the gift of Sabbath rest. Our violation of his design for us in creation has led to our overextension, stress, and exhaustion. The answer is not to do something to escape but to stop and rest in him. Paul exhorts us in Ephesians 5:18-20, "Don't be drunk with wine, because that will ruin your life. Instead, let the Holy Spirit fill and control you. Then you will sing psalms and hymns and spiritual songs among yourselves, making music to the Lord in your hearts. And you will always give thanks for everything to God the Father in the name of our Lord Jesus Christ."

These examples illustrate that we have been given the mind of Christ (see 1 Corinthians 2:16) so that we can see the lie and respond. A caution: Many temptations have a sliver of truth. They may point out legitimate needs in our life, while enticing us to satisfy those needs in illegitimate ways.

TURN TO GOD'S TRUTH

As we've seen, God's Word is the only sure way to combat the lies of evil. Scripture exposes the lies behind temptation and points the way to life. Jesus showed us this in his wilderness temptation, when he answered every temptation with Scripture that conveyed God's principles and priorities for our life (see Matthew 4:1-11). Jesus had soaked his heart and mind in the Word of God. When he was squeezed by evil, the only thing wrung from him was God's Word and truth.

Steve and I saw that Scripture warns that adultery brings destruction (see Proverbs 5:1-14) and calls for faithfulness "to the wife of your youth" (see Proverbs 5:15-23; Malachi 2:13-16). Steve wrote these passages down with the intent of reading them every day. He also shared that God's Word was helping him gain perspective on his situation. What surprised him most was the fact that he was *not* dissatisfied in his marriage. In fact, he was quite happy. But he knew he had been taking so much for granted. He had lost his vision for what a marriage was meant to be. He hadn't been enjoying his wife. He hadn't been appreciating the privilege of sharing life with her. Reading God's Word motivated him to think about how to express affection and give attention to Jenny. "If it matters that much to God," he said, "I guess I'd better take it more seriously!" The best defense, as they say, is a good offense.

One mistake many of us make is expecting instant direction and strength from God's Word. When tempted, we want to turn to a passage that shows us the way out.

God is merciful and may give us answers, but too often we have such a poor grasp of God's Word that evil is able to get a firm grasp on our life.

There is no substitute for spending time daily in Scripture, marinating in the truth. Like the person who immerses herself in another culture in order to learn a foreign language, we learn God's ways best by being immersed in God's Word. It reshapes our thinking and sensitizes our spirit in ways nothing else can. Daily strength comes from daily exercise.

TAKE EVERY THOUGHT CAPTIVE

The third line of defense is to turn from God's truth back to the temptation. Here we follow Paul's counsel: "For though we live in the world, we do not wage war as the world does. The weapons we fight with are not the weapons of the world. On the contrary, they have divine power to demolish strongholds. We demolish arguments and every pretension that sets itself up against the knowledge of God, and we take captive every thought to make it obedient to Christ" (2 Corinthians 10:3-5, NIV).

Sin destroys. There is no such thing as a harmless sin. We must tell ourselves the truth about Satan's designs and about the consequences of sin. In Steve's case this meant replacing fantasies of pleasure with facts, such as the devastating consequences sexual indiscretion would bring upon himself, his wife, their marriage, all their relatives and friends, and his career, as well as the other woman.

To help understand the consequences of sexual sin, we again looked at Scripture, this time at the story of

David and Bathsheba (see 2 Samuel 11–12). The prophet Nathan's rebuke of David for committing adultery with Bathsheba and arranging the death of her husband brings home the fact that *even with repentance and forgiveness, sin sets terrible consequences in motion.* Often, these consequences are not reversed. For David, life was never the same after his sin. "The sword will never depart from your house," said the Lord (2 Samuel 12:10, NIV)—and that's what came to pass.

One specific method for taking our thoughts captive is to use negative imagination to counteract the idealized images that make temptations so inviting. A primary component of temptation is fantasy. The tempted person sees the object of the temptation (whether it is a situation or a person or a material gain) through idealistic lenses. This is simply another aspect of the lie. We must strip away the coverings that conceal the truth, exposing the ugliness beneath. The goal is to make the temptation as undesirable as possible. It's important to note that other people should never be devalued in this process—only the idealization that ensnares the imagination.

Steve began to see that gaining victory over sin begins with ruthlessly considering the consequences of sin. He forced himself to picture the way his wife would react to learning of his adultery. The way he would be shadowed by shame and disgrace. The way he would make a mockery of his faith. These images of the consequences of infidelity were a cold shower on his simmering passion.

Steve also tried to picture the "temptress" in a negative, even repulsive, light. He reminded himself that when he saw her at work, she was dressed in professional clothes with her hair and makeup at their best for the business day. He imagined her greatly aged, in sloppy clothes, and with no makeup. That was a fantasy slayer! He also wrote a series of sentences such as, "How dare she try to hurt my wife like this. It would be a type of murder, causing us unbearable pain. How dare she try to spoil the lives of our children. It would be like letting her barge into our home and take them away. How could she do that to my family?"

More cold showers. Steve was forcing himself to consider the frightening possibilities of "the law of unintended consequences." What starts out as a careless tryst between a man and a woman becomes the stuff of nightmares. Reminding ourself that the attraction we feel to any temptation could prove "fatal"—in countless ways—can do much to counteract the satanic magnetism of sin.

FLEE DANGER AND AVOID TRAPS

The fourth step is to flee temptation and learn to anticipate "dangerous situations" so that no trap can be sprung. Second Timothy 2:22 commands us to flee youthful desires. There are those who think they can withstand temptation, so they refuse to leave a morally perilous situation or relationship. These people remind me of those who insist on staying in the path of a hurricane "just to see what it's like." This invites trouble. Joseph fled from Potiphar's wife, even wiggling out of his coat when she grabbed it (see Genesis 39:12). Reasoned argument and polite actions had failed, so it was the time to dash, not debate.

For Steve, fleeing temptation meant guarding

against flirtatious language and gestures. Although he had to continue working with the woman who was trying to lure him into an adulterous relationship, Steve made a commitment to himself that he would never be alone with her—that he would have someone else around or would be in a public setting whenever they had to work together. And no more lunches with just the two of them. He determined to leave office parties early, letting it be known that he wanted to get home and be with his family. He even determined to leave work and come home immediately if a situation got too intense.

PRAY, PRAY, AND PRAY SOME MORE!

Prayer is listed fifth in this list of steps that are part of resisting temptation, but in fact it should bathe the entire process. After our conversation, I invited Steve to a time of prayer. He prayed first, pouring out his heart to God with a candor and fervency that surprised me. By this time he was completely broken by the situation but also greatly strengthened by our time together. He confessed his sins of flirtation, fantasy, lust, and "mental adultery." Then I prayed a strong prayer of intercession for Steve and Jenny—and for the woman who, like Steve, was trapped in temptation's web. Finally, Steve expressed his forgiveness of her, praying for her to find Jesus Christ and a relationship where godly love could be shared.

Steve and I also committed ourselves to praying for each other daily for the next thirty days. This kind of prayer covenant with another person for a particular situation can be a great support and encouragement.

COMMIT YOURSELF TO CONSISTENT FELLOWSHIP AND ACCOUNTABILITY

The old saying, "There is safety in numbers," has much to recommend it. While preaching on Jesus' temptations in the wilderness, the fourth-century preacher Chrysostom (whose name is Latin for "golden mouth") made the point that the devil especially attacks the lonely (like Eve in the Garden in Genesis 3). When we are in Christian fellowship with others, the devil is not as apt to attack: "Wherefore (let us) be flocking together continually!" Chrysostom exhorted.[1]

Matthew 18:19-20 tells us that when we gather in Jesus' name, the Lord is present in a more powerful way. We also have the encouragement and "reality check" of others who will expose the lies of evil and stop us from giving in to temptation. Steve carried my home and church phone numbers with him so he could call me anytime, day or night.

By the time Steve left my office that night, he seemed to have come through the fire and was ready to stand firm. Several weeks passed, during which time we saw each other in church but didn't have an opportunity to talk. Then we had another committee meeting. Again, I noticed Steve lingering but felt it best to let him approach me in his own time. We walked out to the parking lot together. When everyone else had gone, he said, "Doug, I think you saved my life. The morning after we talked, I gave the woman back her map and key and told her exactly where I stood. I let her know that I am totally committed to my marriage and that I didn't want there to be any confusion about our relationship.

"I feel so great! It's like I closed the biggest deal of my life. No—it's even better! I feel clean. If I had not felt safe telling you, I honestly don't know if I could have lasted."

Steve and I had put in a tremendous amount of effort the evening we had talked and prayed together. I am convinced that it was worth every moment—especially when I think of the countless *years* of agony that dozens and possibly hundreds of people were spared because Steve was equipped to battle temptation.

Many of us have often read, and even memorized, I Corinthians 10:13, "No temptation has overtaken you that is not common to man. God is faithful, and he will not let you be tempted beyond your strength, but *with the temptation will also provide the way of escape, that you may be able to endure it*" (RSV, emphasis added). By God's grace and the power of the Holy Spirit, we are not helpless victims of temptation or pawns of the world and the flesh. We can stand strong in Christ.

I am learning that, even as we pray the Lord's Prayer, "and lead us not into temptation, but deliver us from evil," we can also pray, "Lord, lead us *out of* temptation." When we see God do this, we realize just how great God is!

NOTES

1. Frederick Dale Bruner, *The Christ Book* (Waco: Word Books, 1987), 103.

CHAPTER EIGHT

Confronting the Powers of Darkness

The purpose of this chapter is to give an overview of how we can confront the devil and his demons through such practices as deliverance prayer. *Deliverance* is the process of freeing a person who is oppressed by evil spirits. Deliverance prayer is usually distinguished from *solemn exorcism,* which is a formal ecclesiastical prayer to free a person who is not just oppressed, but actually possessed by an evil spirit.[1]

Awareness of demon possession and exorcism increased in the last generation primarily because of movies such as *The Exorcist* and *Rosemary's Baby.* There are some fascinating serious studies of demon possession such as the book by Malachi Martin, *Hostage to the Devil,* (Harper & Row, 1976). But the reality of demonic influence on a less dramatic level than full possession is less well known.

As we discuss how to confront the demonic forces that are at work in this world, it is important to keep in mind all the material that we have covered in the previous chapters. Deliverance is simply one aspect of spiritual warfare—not the whole story. If we put all our emphasis on the demonic, we distort reality and often lure people away from faith and into fascination with evil. There is great danger here—both to ourselves and to those we seek to serve. A careless or cavalier attitude can cause harm in multiple ways. People may either be intimidated by the prospect of demonization, or they may evade responsibility for repenting from their sin by blaming the devil.

We must keep our focus on Christ, our mind rooted in God's Word, our heart humbled before the Lord, and our love for the person being influenced by forces of darkness uppermost in our actions. We must be neither timid nor proud. Instead, we must act out of love and obedience—with the authority that has been given us as followers of Jesus Christ, empowered by the Holy Spirit.

While some are tempted to see demons behind every problem, my study and experience have led me to be much more conservative. I have seen a broad consensus emerging across a number of historic Christian traditions, a consensus that is balanced, biblical, and consistently loving and pastoral. In keeping with this consensus, I've concluded that there are more than enough problems in our lives due primarily to the flesh and the world—there's no need to jump to the conclusion that everything is caused by the devil or demons. The forces of evil get plenty of help from us! But we must also be equipped to confront the forces of darkness with confidence and authority. Having said this, we can now examine the nature of evil and the power of the gospel to overcome it.

THE NATURE OF EVIL INFLUENCE OVER OUR LIVES

Many of us have an "all or nothing" concept of demon influence: Either a person is possessed by demons or is free of their control. But that is inaccurate. The actual term used in Scripture to describe a person afflicted with demons is that they are *demonized*. It appears that there can be levels of demonic influence in a person's life. Any level less than possession is referred to in Scripture as *demonization*. This term encompasses what might be viewed as several levels of evil influence over a person. In looking at accounts of Jesus' confrontations with demons, we see that he was able to cast out some of them with a simple command (Mark 1:25). Casting out others, however, required prayer and fasting (Mark 9:29).

Partial demonic influence over a personality has been described as affliction, oppression, bondage, the presence of strongholds, or demonization. Levels of demonic influence are perhaps best considered on a spectrum from low to high. Chuck Kraft recommends using a scale from one to ten, with one signifying the weakest level of influence (or strength of attachment) and ten the strongest. "The Gospels show Jesus casting out demons with a strength of attachment at a level of 9 or 10," says Kraft. "Most of those we regularly encounter are, however, in the 1, 2, or 3 category. They usually go quietly when commanded to in the name of Jesus."[2]

A demonizing influence is usually over certain areas of a person's life. Some have compared it to a military invasion of a city. Even when friendly forces occupy and control most of the city, isolated areas can remain under enemy domination. Examples of the effects of demonic influence include a deaf-and-dumb spirit (Mark 9:25), a spirit of divination (Acts 16:16), a spirit of infirmity (Luke 13:11), and a seducing or deceiving spirit (1 Timothy 4:1).

The fact that someone is demonized does not mean he or she is without faith or is lacking salvation. Unlike demon *possession,* which is not possible in Christians because believers are indwelt by the Holy Spirit (see Ephesians 1:13-14 and Romans 8:9-11), demonization *can* affect God's children.

The level of demonic influence in a person's life may be related to his or her own choices, especially in dealing with past behavior and hurts. Or it may be the result of a curse that goes back for generations. In Cheryl's case (described in the first chapter), the demon influencing her claimed to have been sent as the result of a curse made against the thirteenth generation of her family by a witch who was burned at the stake in the 1600s in New England. In all candor, I can't say I necessarily affirm that claim, but the Bible and others' experience do demonstrate that curses have real consequences.

Francis MacNutt writes, "I find that possession is rare, but people who are 'demonized,' who are attacked or *oppressed* by demonic forces, are a relatively common occurrence."[3]

Neil Anderson talks about three levels of bondage. On the first level, the believer leads a fairly normal life but is "wrestling with a steady barrage of sinful thoughts on the inside: lust, envy, greed, hatred, apathy, etc." He estimates that 65 percent of all Christians live at this level of spiritual conflict, subject to the fiery darts of the enemy against their thinking. The second level is seen in those who can distinguish between their own thoughts and strange, "evil" voices that seem to over-power them. Counseling and earnest efforts at self-discipline do nothing to improve their situation. An-derson estimates that 15 percent of all believers fall into this category of demon influence. At the third level, the individual "has lost control and hears voices inside his mind which tell him what to think, say, and do." An-derson estimates that 5 percent of Christians live at this level of deception and control.[4]

My personal counsel is to sit loosely with the concept of demonization, being willing to accept the fact that the demonic may interfere with our lives. We do not need to be constantly fearful about demon influence. The fact is that evil forces actually lose much power when we confront them with a nonanxious response. Their primary power lies in fear and hiddenness.

WHAT ARE INDICATIONS OF DEMONIC INTERFERENCE?

How do we know if demonic forces are at work in a situ-ation? How can we distinguish demonic influence from the temptations of the world or the flesh—or from psy-chological disturbance?

Francis MacNutt cites three primary indicators of de-monic influence. The first is the presence of compulsive or addictive behavior. We must be cautious, however, not to attribute all addictive or compulsive behavior to de-monic sources. The proper approach to many compulsions may be repentance, self-discipline, counseling and medication, prayer for healing, or prayer for inner healing from wounds of the past. If, however, there is no progress after normal channels of ministry, behavioral change, and therapy have been pursued, the possibility of demonic interference should be considered.

Second, the affected persons themselves often have some sense of demonic interference. This is not always the case, but they may have strong impressions of evil, such as persistent evil dreams or memories of occult practices and experiences of evil. As mentioned by Neil Anderson, they may hear or have strong impressions of evil voices or messages seemingly coming out of nowhere. "They're very different from my 'normal' bad thoughts or fantasies," one man told me. "These come in the middle of Bible study, prayer, or worship and are absolutely obscene, unlike anything I could have imagined."

Third, God may give someone discernment, either through rational thought processes or by a gift of the Spirit, that there is demonization at work.

While it can sometimes be difficult to recognize certain levels of demonic influence, actual demon possession seems to be more easily recognized because of the extreme expressions of abnormal behavior and other manifestations of evil involved. The Roman [Catholic] Ritual of Exorcism lists some signs of demon possession: "When the subject speaks unknown languages with many words or understands unknown languages; when he clearly knows about things that are distant or hidden; when he shows physical strength far above his age or normal condition."[5]

Two essential principles should be kept in mind when "diagnosing" demonization or demon possession. First, it is imperative that any diagnosis be considered with the prayerful counsel of spiritually mature people who have studied this matter. Second, all conversations and explorations must be conducted in a spirit of love, grace, and nonjudgmental support for the afflicted person. Great harm can be done by attributing a person's problems to demons when other factors are the real cause. Also, believers who are being harassed by demons need continual assurance of their worth and identity in Christ, along with the truth that they are not themselves evil, unclean, or unworthy. They need to be reminded again and again that this was the very reason Jesus came—to set us free from the bondage imposed by Satan and his evil forces (see I John 3:8).

AVENUES OF ENTRANCE

How does a demonic presence gain entrance or influence? Are we powerless against demons? Do they come against our will? Do we somehow invite them to come into our life?

Passages such as Ephesians 4:26-27 give us clues that demons may gain a foothold in our life through our behavior. Frankly, I have not been able to draw a direct cause-and-effect relationship between behavior and demonization. We must remind ourselves again and again, there is much we don't understand here. Still, there are some basic guidelines in Scripture that can inform us. There seem to be five primary entry points that may leave us open to demonic influence.

First, deliberate and unconfessed sin can become a stronghold for evil. When we choose to defy God and spurn his commands, we take evil's side. It's like opening the gates to a city at night. You may intend to let only one person in, but many others sneak in unnoticed. When we let down our spiritual guard, we make way for unclean forces to enter. Sins of money, sex, and power are among the most common avenues of entrance.[6]

Activities and attitudes such as greed, ambition, lust, adultery, pornography, homosexuality, substance abuse, pride, anger, and ambition make us vulnerable. Any sinful activity we engage in, thinking it will be a one-time experience, may actually bind us for a much longer term.

Second, occult and cultic practices and other religions are open invitations to demonic influence. (Neil Anderson's "Non-Christian Experience Inventory" in his book *The Bondage Breaker* gives a comprehensive list of practices that invite demonic influence.) For some reason, we have varying degrees of susceptibility to evil. Some can participate in occult or non-Christian practices with little effect, while some who merely dabble in them are overcome. The best advice is to renounce all such practices and associations.

Third, sins committed against us can also open the way to evil influence. Abuse in all its forms has horrible consequences—even though the victim had nothing to do with bringing abuse upon himself. But the good news is that God can break the power of abuse and sin, setting the captive free. I once counseled a woman who as a young girl had been dedicated to a demon by a witches' coven. The abuse she suffered is unspeakable—in fact, I wish I had never heard her story. But she and her husband saw the power of God break through, overcoming the darkness.

The fourth way into bondage is through a curse. A curse may be the result of anger, revenge, or retribution, or it may be a way of ensuring compliance with a "deal," such as dedicating a life to the service of evil.

Fifth, bondage to evil can be passed down through generations. Exodus 34:6-7 affirms God's boundless love but also warns us that the punishment for sins may be passed down to succeeding generations. Just as the *punishment* for sin can be passed through the generations, so can the *vulnerability* to sin and evil. This "law of the generations" need not be viewed as God's active retribution for sin but can be seen as the natural and logical consequences of sin and evil continuing over time.

Nevertheless, we may need to break the law of generations by praying for forgiveness and for release from the sins of our parents and ancestors. This was one of the most important undertakings of Ezra as he sought to reestablish the nation of Israel following their exile (see Ezra 9 and 10 and also Nehemiah 9). In our age of individualism, we often lose sight of our corporate interrelatedness, not simply in our contemporary community, but with previous generations as well. It is fascinating in this regard that the early church practiced exorcism of all new converts. This concept is reflected in the Episcopal liturgy to this day.

These entry points need to be addressed early in the process of helping a person seek release from bondage to evil—a process that is dealt with thoroughly in Neil Anderson's book *The Bondage Breaker*. I would describe Anderson's approach to confronting demonic influence as closing the doorways to evil (entry points), cleansing the "house," and filling it with the Lord's positive remedy for each negative point of entry. Eliminating strongholds in our life is the first step in confronting the demonic in our life and in the lives of those to whom we're ministering. Some people believe that in addition to the entry points listed above, there are certain geographic locations that are strongholds of demons known as territorial spirits. Frank Peretti's novels *This Present Darkness* and *Piercing the Darkness* present vivid images of demonic powers that have jurisdiction over certain areas. The view that there are indeed territorial spirits has been taken very seriously by people such as Peter Wagner of Fuller Theological Seminary, John Dawson of YWAM (Youth With A Mission), and others in missionary movements. The scriptural basis for this view is rooted in Daniel 10:13, which gives an account of the "spirit-prince of the kingdom of Persia" who blocked the way of the angelic one sent to tell Daniel his prayer had been heard.

I have heard credible missionaries testify to having experienced intense spiritual resistance to evangelistic attempts in certain towns and even certain streets. When attempting to speak to people in one location, they would encounter hostility; but when they spoke to *those same people* in another location they would find them receptive. Some groups are doing "spiritual mapping" of targeted areas to discern the "dominant spirit" of a particular locale.

There is a great deal of debate over this whole idea. Calvin Miller articulates the thoughts of many who are skeptical. "For instance," he says, "one biblical idea that has been somewhat overblown is the idea that demons are territorial. . . . But the practice of pursuing these 'ruling angels' often runs away with the temptation to see demons everywhere. This preoccupation can foster a negative intrigue—with evil that is prone to eliminate the believer's positive focus on Christ."[7]

Miller has a good point. On the other hand, it is interesting to note that the Roman Ritual that was developed from A.D. 200 through the 1600s contains a ritual "for the exorcism of places." No matter where we land theologically, it is certainly appropriate to call God's blessing upon our homes and to dedicate our special places to him. Whether or not demons have authority over particular areas, we need to acknowledge that they can interfere in the activities of this world.

METHODS OF CONFRONTING DEMONIC FORCES

There are two primary approaches to dealing with evil spirits. While on the surface these approaches seem quite different, there are actually many similarities between them. Often, a particular situation lends itself to one approach or the other. A basic knowledge of both approaches can help in deciding which approach is most effective for a certain situation or ministry.

POWER ENCOUNTERS AND TRUTH ENCOUNTERS

Neil Anderson and the late John Wimber represent two different contemporary methods in deliverance ministry. The "signs and wonders" school, which is based on John Wimber's approach and also includes Chuck Kraft and C. Peter Wagner, has centered on the "power encounter"—in which an evil spirit or demon is confronted directly and ordered from a demonized person. This often involves "dialogue" with the demon and draws on the power of the Holy Spirit to exorcise the person. The Roman Ritual of Exorcism actually follows this method. "In practice, the flow of the text [of the ritual] is broken by dialogues between exorcist and Evil Spirit. . . . Questions [the exorcist] must ask the possessing Evil Spirit are, for example: the number and name of the possessing spirits; when they entered the possessed; why they entered him; and other questions of the same kind."[8]

Neil Anderson takes the approach of shining the light of truth to drive out the darkness of evil. He has the demonized or demon-possessed person speak the truth, renouncing sins and occult practices. These verbal prayers of confession and truth telling exorcise the demon(s) without any direct confrontation with the demon itself.

These two approaches do not need to be exclusive or antagonistic. Both have numerous testimonies to their effectiveness. A careful study of both approaches also reveals many points of overlap, so my own advice is to be armed with the tools and weapons of both methods in order to be as fully equipped as possible. For a detailed presentation of Neil Anderson's method, see his book *The Bondage Breaker*. The model of deliverance prayer we are going to examine here is based on biblical principles that are presented in what I would call the more "traditional" method. This method is found in both the Roman Ritual and power-encounter formats.

PRINCIPLES OF DELIVERANCE MINISTRY

We should not be "demon seekers," looking for evil spirits in every problem we encounter. The Lord should be our preoccupation and our new nature in Christ our focus. But when we discern that the demonic is at work, we must know how to respond. We should come against the evil spirit in the name, authority, and Spirit of Jesus Christ. Generally speaking, we should follow the model for prayer ministry presented earlier, while keeping the following additional principles in mind.

First, demons are expelled in Jesus' name (see Matthew 7:22; Mark 9:38-39; Acts 4:30; 16:18). There is no greater name in all creation than the name of Jesus, the Son of God who died, rose from the dead, and sits at the right hand of the Father. Demons may challenge our authority, accusing us of sinfulness, worthlessness, and presumption. If so, we answer them by agreeing that apart from Christ we can do nothing (see John

15:5), but that as believers in Jesus Christ, we share in his authority. We stand on the promise made to Peter for all believers who confess Christ: "On this rock I will build my church, and the gates of Hades will not overcome it. I will give you the keys of the kingdom of heaven; whatever you bind on earth will be bound in heaven, and whatever you loose on earth will be loosed in heaven" (Matthew 16:18-19, NIV).

Second, while we can command demons to identify themselves and their function (see Mark 5:6-9), it is not advisable to give them attention through extensive conversation and bargaining. Naming seems to have a place because of the biblical concept that to use a name is to have some measure of power or influence over a being. Adam was given the privilege of naming creatures as an expression of his dominion (see Genesis 2:19-20). Naming demons exposes them and their assignments. It shines the light of truth, breaking the power of darkness and hiddenness. Since demons are commonly named by their activities, we can often simply call them by a word that relates to what the prayed-for person identifies as a problem.

Third, we should be aware of such evasive tactics of hiding, tricking, lying, and distracting, and even direct attack (see Acts 19:13-20). Demons can seem like rascally, mischievous children, taunting and toying with us. We must not be deceived when they seem to give in—they may have simply gone into hiding, hoping we will let them alone. We must persist, calling them from hiding by the power of the Holy Spirit. We should also forbid them to lie or to cause harm to any of the people involved (see "binding" below). They may even try to flatter us, but we must resist this foolishness and stay focused.

Finally, we must always be compassionate, respecting the dignity of people in need of deliverance ministry. There is no need to shout or exhibit dramatic displays of power. Such histrionics can actually be harmful to the person for whom we are praying. They can also raise the level of antagonism and resistance. A calm, quiet, authoritative demeanor is most becoming. What's more, as David Du Plessis has warned, there is an occupational hazard of exorcists becoming infected by what they combat; they may become harsh and judgmental over the years.[9]

DELIVERANCE PRAYER

There are four basic elements to deliverance. While they are presented sequentially here, it may be necessary to move back and forth among them, depending on the dynamics of the encounter.

SCRIPTURAL COVERING

Root your authority and statements in the Word of God, not your own wisdom or other human authority. Reading the Bible "softens the soil," so to speak, beginning the process of release. Common texts for this are:

- The Lord's Prayer (Matthew 6:9-13), especially "deliver us from evil"
- Psalm 54, which can be turned into a prayer of petition for the person

Gospel passages on the authority of Jesus and his victory over evil are:

- Mark 16:15-18 on the authority Jesus gave his followers over evil
- Luke 10:17-20 on the victory of Jesus' followers over demons and the defeat of Satan
- Luke 11:14-22 on Jesus' authority over Beelzebub
- John 1:1-12 on the incarnate Word

PRAYER OF PROTECTION AND BINDING

As noted already, Jesus' followers have been given authority to bind and loose. In deliverance, in addition to protecting ourselves with the full armor of God, it is especially important to bind evil from destructive, distracting, and unclean practices (such as vomiting or defecating). We do this by commanding the evil spirits to be bound and lose their power to resist. A sample prayer would be:

> *By the authority of the Lord Jesus Christ, you are bound.*
> *In Jesus' name we forbid you to cause any harm or any*
> *uncleanness. You are not to choke or cause sickness or resist*
> *the power of the Lord Jesus Christ. You are to tell the truth.*
> *In Jesus' name, we forbid you to hide. You are exposed by the*
> *light of Christ.*

THE PRAYER OF COMMAND

This is a very simple one-sentence prayer, but may require more than one pronouncement to secure results. The following is a traditional prayer of deliverance described by Francis MacNutt.[10]

The prayer is:

In the name of Jesus Christ I command you, spirit of _____ to be gone, without causing any harm, and I send you to the feet of Jesus. Cause no harm on the way and never return.

Let's look at the elements of this prayer. First, we act in the name of Jesus. Deliverance is possible only through his authority and power. Notice that we *command* the demon—we do not ask *it* if *it* would be so pleased as to go! One person told me, "Shoo the demons out, like telling a cat to scat off the porch." Again, this can be done in a calm, quiet voice, without histrionics.

We are reminded of the importance of our standing under the Lord's authority in Jude 1:9: "But even Michael, one of the mightiest of the angels, did not dare accuse Satan of blasphemy, but simply said, 'The Lord rebuke you.' (This took place when Michael was arguing with Satan about Moses' body.)"

This passage, which alludes to a traditional account probably drawn from a book (not in the Bible) called *The Assumption of Moses,* portrays Michael's expression of humble submission under Christ along with his bold declaration of authority in Christ over the evil one.

Second, we name the spirit (see Mark 5:9 and Mark 9:25). As mentioned above, this is a means of exercising authority and control. If the name is not coming, we may use a generic designation, like "unclean spirit," or "evil spirit, by whatever name."

Third, we command the spirit to leave—to depart, to be gone, to come out. This is clearly the model of Jesus (see Mark 1:25; Mark 9:25). It is the essence of deliverance—delivering a person from the oppressive influence of an evil pest.

Fourth, we command the spirit to leave without causing any harm to anyone. This was already addressed under the subject of binding, but it is good to reiterate. You don't want others in the room or area to be harassed by the evil spirit. This step is sort of a leash, restraining the spirit as it is dismissed to Jesus' command.

Fifth, we send the spirit to Jesus, in order for Jesus to determine its fate. I have heard of people sending or threatening to send demons to the abyss, but that seems to be presumptuous. Jesus is their ultimate judge.

PRAYER OF BLESSING

I picture this step as filling the newly empty person to overflowing with the cleaning, refreshing love and grace of the Lord. The prayer of blessing has two aspects.

First, we bless the person who has been delivered. I personally take time to assure the person in prayer that God has worked and that he or she should celebrate this day of liberation. I often pray, "Almighty God, we praise you for your victory and seal this time in the name of the Father, the Son, and the Holy Spirit. Let no spirit of self-condemnation, embarrassment, or accusation enter."

Second, we invite the person to pray for those who've been part of the process of deliverance. This is important in affirming the person's faith and newfound freedom, as well as acknowledging the fact that we are mutually encouraged by each other's faith. The prayed-for person has taken a major step of faith by surrendering to this whole process. We want to affirm that we can receive blessing from him or her and that he or she is fully qualified to minister in the Lord's name. This is a time to be savored, a very special time of thanksgiving and worship.

The glory of God is a holy alchemy of turning evil things into the means for deeper experiences of his power and grace. His light shines more brightly in the darkness, his power is displayed more fully in our weakness, and his love is known most completely in contrast to evil. While we would never go searching for spiritual conflict, we need not fear it. For nothing can separate us from the love of God in Christ Jesus our Lord.

NOTES

1. Francis MacNutt, *Healing* (Notre Dame: Ave Maria Press, 1974), 208.

2. Charles Kraft, *Christianity With Power* (Ann Arbor, Mich.: Vine Books, 1989), 129.

3. MacNutt, *Healing*, 216.

4. Neil T. Anderson, *The Bondage Breaker* (Eugene, Oreg.: Harvest House, 1990), 107–108.

5. Malachi Martin, *Hostage to the Devil: The Possession and Exorcism of Five Living Americans* (New York: Harper & Row Publishers, 1976), 460.

6. Calvin Miller, *Disarming the Darkness* (Grand Rapids: Zondervan, 1998), 91–156.

7. Ibid., 20–21.

8. Martin, *Hostage to the Devil*, 459–62.

9. MacNutt, *Healing*, 225.

10. MacNutt, 224–26.

CHAPTER NINE

Holy Battle Strategies

The more we are aware of the spiritual battles going on around us, the more we experience the power of God's peace—and the peace of God's power. We do not fear evil; instead we are prepared to face it in the overcoming strength and authority of Jesus Christ.

For the maturing believer, spiritual warfare becomes a way of life. We are always in a state of spiritual readiness, guarding against the assaults of the world, the flesh, and the devil. This does not mean that we are anxious, living in fear of attack. Instead, we live in joy and freedom, confident that nothing can separate us from the Lord. We know who we are in Christ, the greatness of power in those of us who believe, and the resources he has given us.

As we conclude our study of spiritual warfare, we are going to look at some stories of actual military battles recorded in the Bible—battles that illustrate key principles of spiritual warfare.

TRUST THE LORD TO FIGHT THE BATTLE

We are most vulnerable to defeat when we forget that we really are engaged in the *Lord's* battle, not our own. Even as a soldier fights an enemy on behalf of his nation, so we stand against evil as citizens of God's kingdom. Moses and the people of Israel were taught this lesson early on. If you've studied the story of their escape from Egypt (told in Exodus 7–14), you know that the dramatic liberation of the Israelites from Pharaoh followed the death of all the firstborn Egyptian male children. This liberation, however, was short-lived because Pharaoh sent his armies to pursue the Israelites and bring them back. Within days of their departure from Egypt, Moses and the Israelites were trapped—with the sea on one side, the mountains on another, and Pharaoh's armies fast approaching. There was nowhere to go! The people cried out in despair, "Why did you bring us out here to die in the wilderness? Weren't there enough graves for us in Egypt? Why did you make us leave? Didn't we tell you to leave us alone while we were still in Egypt? Our Egyptian slavery was far better than dying out here in the wilderness!" (Exodus 14:11-12).

Understandably, the people were overwhelmed. But Moses taught them a lesson that they would have to learn time and again—when you're fighting on God's side, he will take care of you. "But Moses told the people, 'Don't be afraid. Just stand where you are and watch the Lord rescue you. The Egyptians that you see today will never be seen again. The Lord himself will fight for you. You won't have to lift a finger in your defense!'" (Exodus

14:13-14). Moses was right, of course, as the Lord parted the waters of the sea for the Israelites to cross over, then closed up the waters after Pharaoh's army had charged into the sea.

Our starting point in spiritual warfare is faith that relies on God's care and God's protection. He promises that, if we seek first his kingdom (see Matthew 6:33), he will provide all we need. This includes protection as well as provision. When we realize that the battle belongs to the Lord, a "dead end" becomes the beginning of God's greatest victory. He has resources and strategies we can never imagine. Therefore, we do not need to be intimidated by evil.

How does this principle work in our lives? Consider the situation of Bob and Denise, who entered a business partnership with several other people they later found out were unscrupulous. When they became aware of this, Bob and Denise said they wanted out of the business. Their partners threatened them, asserting they were liable for any inappropriate actions and that, consequently, they had better cooperate. Seeing no human way out of their situation, Bob and Denise began to pray. "What happened next could only have been God's work," said Denise later. One of their business partners had other interests that came under investigation by a government agency. In the course of the investigation, the two other partners brought charges against each other in such a way that Bob and Denise were able to extricate themselves from the business without any charges or violation of their integrity. Although the answer came after much heartache, this story is one of many that leave me encouraged by the way in which God continually brings victory when there seems to be no way out.

FOCUS ON WORSHIP, NOT WARFARE

Satan's primary purpose in spiritual warfare is to divert us from worship and intimate fellowship with God, and the forces of evil use warfare as their primary weapon to divert us from worship. Worship is the chief activity of heaven (see Revelation 4–5) and the most hated activity of hell. Rather than fighting evil directly when it attacks, we need to turn to the Lord in worship. The Lord draws near to those who worship. He honors those who take refuge in the temple of praise.

> *What mighty praise, O God,*
> *belongs to you in Zion.*
> *We will fulfill our vows to you,*
> *for you answer our prayers,*
> *and to you all people will come.*
> *Though our hearts are filled with sins,*
> *you forgive them all.*
> *What joy for those you choose to bring near,*
> *those who live in your holy courts.*
> *What joys await us*
> *inside your holy Temple.*
> *You faithfully answer our prayers with awesome deeds,*
> *O God our savior.*
> *You are the hope of everyone on earth,*
> *even those who sail on distant seas.* (Psalm 65:1-5)

My favorite illustration of this point is found in 2 Chronicles 20. Jehoshaphat and the Israelites were being attacked by the Moabites, Ammonites, and Meunites. Jehoshaphat immediately called the people to prayer. He begins his prayer with glorious praise (see 2 Chronicles 20:6) and then "reminds" the Lord and all who are gathered of the mighty work and great promises of God (2 Chronicles 20:7-11). Then he offers his plea: "We are powerless against this mighty army that is about to attack us. We do not know what to do, but we are looking to you for help" (2 Chronicles 20:12).

What did God do? He called them to gather together for worship, and here's what happened: The choir singers literally marched in front of the Israelite army, singing and praising the Lord. And then: "At the moment they began to sing and give praise, the Lord caused the armies of Ammon, Moab, and Mount Seir to start fighting among themselves. The armies of Moab and Ammon turned against their allies from Mount Seir and killed every one of them. After they had finished off the army of Seir, they turned on each other." (2 Chronicles 20:22-23).

In other words, as the people of God sang praises, the enemy armies turned against and destroyed each other—without ever coming near the Israelites!

When we turn to God in worship, God turns our enemies against each other. The very thing that makes them enemies makes them vulnerable to destructive forces that will turn against themselves—they carry the seeds of their own destruction within.

I saw this principle at work when a man I'll call Tom was being drained by a frivolous and expensive lawsuit filed against him by an angry client. That Tom had acted with integrity was confirmed by many who were close to the case. Still the case dragged on, weighing on him emotionally and draining his resources through legal fees. After years of battling the case, Tom asked a group of people to soak the situation in prayer. They gathered together in his home several times for singing and prayer. "I just need to get my eyes on God," Tom told the group, "and off this situation." After a few weeks, one of the group members came across information that eventually led to the dismissal of the case against Tom. "All I know," said Tom later, "is that this client seemed to have me over a barrel, until I decided to change my focus to praise and trusting the Lord."

TRUST GOD'S WORD, NOT YOUR OWN PERCEPTIONS

We are often defeated because we look at the situation *around* us instead of looking to the Lord *above* us. The story of Joshua and Caleb's spying out the Promised Land reminds us that we must trust the Lord's word, not our own perceptions. In Numbers 13, men from each of the Israelite tribes scouted the land and returned with the proverbial good news/bad news. The good news was that the land was even better than they could have hoped for. The bad news:

"We can't go up against them! They are stronger than we are!" So they spread discouraging reports about the land among the Israelites: "The land we explored will swallow up any who go to live there. All the people we saw were huge. We even saw giants there, the descendants of Anak. We felt like grasshoppers next to them, and that's what we looked like to them!" (Numbers 13:31-33)

Blessings rarely come without giants. God knew there were giants when he gave the promise of the land. Part of the promise lay in trusting that God would secure a victory that could come only through his power.

When we view our circumstances from our human perspective, we often allow problems and obstacles to overshadow the True Reality. Like the disciples who could not imagine how to feed five thousand people (see Luke 9:10-17), all we see is the hungry crowd of human need instead of the limitless power of divine resources. Spiritual maturity comes as we act on the faith that God is not limited to what we can see.

Caleb and Joshua saw the giants but concentrated on God's word of promise:

"The land we explored is a wonderful land! And if the Lord is pleased with us, he will bring us safely into that land and give it to us. It is a rich land flowing with milk and honey, and he will give it to us! Do not rebel against the Lord, and don't be afraid of the people of the land. They are only helpless prey to us! They have no protection, but the Lord is with us! Don't be afraid of them!" (Numbers 14:7-9)

The principle here is that we can renew our minds and be victorious by looking at life from God's perspective, seeing beyond the bluff and bluster of the world. Paul says that we are to be transformed by the renewal of our minds (see Romans 12:2). This fact of spiritual life is the key to breaking free from the lies of fear that paralyze us. As Paul says elsewhere, "we walk by faith, not by sight," (2 Corinthians 5:7, RSV).

Trusting God's Word is essential for fighting the temptations of the world and the flesh, which can include perceptions like "Things will never change," "I will always fail," or "They will always hurt me." Instead of buying into these perceptions, which erode our confidence and bring defeat every time, we need to take our stand on the promises of God. And though many of us may never have a direct encounter with the demonic, such encounters are prime examples of the need to trust the Lord's Word, not our own perceptions. Horror stories and Hollywood movies have terrorized us with portrayals of evil—but Satan is a defeated enemy, quivering in the throes of death. Though he looks like a giant, God is far, far greater!

UNLEASH THE POWER OF PRAYER PARTNERS

Too often we try to take on the enemy alone because we are reluctant to expose our needs to others—or embarrassed to ask for help. But God calls us into partnership, especially in spiritual battles. Jesus sent his disciples out in pairs (see Mark 6:7) so that they could be a source of strength and encouragement to each other.

A vivid illustration of our mutual interdependence in prayer and warfare is the story of Moses, Aaron, and Hur (Exodus 17:8-16). Even Moses, with all his spiritual depth and power, needed Aaron and Hur to fulfill his prayer ministry and bring victory in battle against the Amalekites. In this fascinating story, the outcome of the battle is directly linked to prayer. Moses stood on a hill overlooking the battle, lifting up his hands while holding the staff of God in them (upraised hands were a common posture for prayers requesting God's special help—see Psalm 63:4; 1 Timothy 2:8). When Moses' hands were lifted with his staff in prayer, the Israelites would win. When Moses tired and lowered his arms, Israel would start losing. So Aaron and Hur stood on either side of him, holding his hands up, until sunset. When the Israelite army triumphed, it was clear that the power of God, not the skill of the warriors, had made the difference.

The point of this passage is not simply the importance of prayer, but of joining together with others in prayer—something Jesus called us to do in Matthew 18:19-20. Though the Lord is always with us, his presence is manifested in special ways when we pray with other believers. Prayer with others often releases additional encouragement, assurance, testimonies of God's faithfulness, insight, accountability, and faith. We especially need to join with others when conflict, including spiritual conflict, is intense. Intense battles—like the one between the Israelites and the Amalekites, fierce warriors who threatened to crush God's fledgling nation—require extensive prayer support.

Who holds up your hands? Who can you call, anytime, day or night, for prayer and support? If you don't have such a person, begin praying now for God to provide one.

How could God use you to encourage the spiritual leaders in your life, such as your pastor, teachers, and youth and children's leaders? Consider one specific commitment you could make to hold them up in regular prayer.

Never go into battle alone, and never go without prayer.

RELY ON GOD'S LOGIC

The Lord reminds us in Isaiah 55:8-9, " 'My thoughts are completely different from yours,' " says the Lord. " 'And my ways are far beyond anything you could imagine. For just as the heavens are higher than the earth, so are my ways higher than your ways and my thoughts higher than your thoughts.' " When we enter spiritual conflict, we are tempted to try to resolve the situation with human resources and logic. Yet that usually ends in failure. We must learn to rely on God's logic.

The story of Gideon's going into battle against the Midianites shows us that God does not necessarily follow earthly logic and reason (see Judges 7). In this case, God did more with less. When Gideon amassed 32,000 warriors for battle, God winnowed the number down to three hundred. Why? The reason is given in Judges 7:2: "The Lord said to Gideon, 'You have too many warriors with you. If I let all of you fight the Midianites, the Israelites will boast to me that they saved themselves by their own strength.' "

God's logic humbles human pride. As Paul teaches us in 1 Corinthians 1:27-31:

God deliberately chose things the world considers foolish in order to shame those who think they are wise. And he chose those who are powerless to shame those who are powerful. God chose things despised by the world, things counted as nothing at all, and used them to bring to nothing what the world considers important, so that no one can ever boast in the presence of God. . . . As the Scriptures say, "The person who wishes to boast should boast only of what the Lord has done."

God works in ways that inspire awe and gratitude.

SEEK THE LORD'S HONOR

There's something energizing about standing up for what we believe is right. We feel a sense of virtue that enables us to be selfless and sacrificial. This was the secret to the chivalry of noble medieval knights. The essence of spiritual warfare is the fact that we are standing up for the Lord's honor and sacrificing ourselves in some way for the Lord's people.

When we pray the Lord's Prayer (see Matthew 6:9-13, KJV), we begin with the first petition, "Hallowed be thy name." We are praying that God's greatness will be respected, that his name will be honored, and that he will be glorified through worship and obedience. When we understand both the love and majesty of the Lord God Almighty, we actually wince when we hear his name used in vain or see him defied and mocked.

Such was David's reaction as he witnessed the blasphemy of Goliath (see 1 Samuel 17). David was intensely committed to the Lord's honor. He wanted to guard the Lord's name and to promote the reputation of God's people. He was seeking neither personal glory nor personal gain. The story of David and Goliath models a number of important principles of spiritual warfare:

- Rely on God's resources and strength.
- Victory lies not in the size of the body but in the size of the heart.
- Our battle strategy isn't a matter of brute force but of spiritual finesse.
- Don't let the enemy's size scare you! Outward appearances only intimidate us if we take our eyes off the Lord.

These are important principles—but just as important is the motivation behind them. David proclaims the most important motive and goal of spiritual warfare: to withstand any who defy the living God (see 1 Samuel 17:26). Spiritual warfare is not just a means to self-protection—it is the expression of our commitment to honor and glorify the Lord, resisting all who are traitors to God's kingdom.

RESIST THE SNARE OF SPIRITUAL PRIDE

God's blessing must never be taken for granted. When we've tasted victory, we may actually be close to defeat. Those who have found favor with the Lord are in danger of letting down their guard. This was Josiah's mistake.

Josiah was one of the godly kings of Judah, as we see in 2 Chronicles 34:2: "He did what was pleasing in the Lord's sight and followed the example of his ancestor David. He did not turn aside from doing what was right." Josiah honored God through his reforms, ridding Judah of pagan practices and restoring the worship of the Lord. But when Pharaoh Neco of Egypt and his army traveled through Judah to fight against the Assyrians at Carchemish, Josiah went out to fight him. Pharaoh warned him to stay out of the battle. He sent ambassadors to Josiah with this message:

> "What do you want with me, king of Judah? I have no quarrel with you today! I only want to fight the nation with which I am at war. And God has told me to hurry! Do not interfere with God, who is with me, or he will destroy you."

> But Josiah refused to listen to Neco, to whom God had indeed spoken, and he would not turn back. Instead, he led his army into battle on the plain of Megiddo. He laid aside his royal robes so the enemy would not recognize him. But the enemy archers hit King Josiah with their arrows and wounded him. He cried out to his men, "Take me from the battle, for I am badly wounded!"

> So they lifted Josiah out of his chariot and placed him in another chariot. Then they brought him back to Jerusalem, where he died. (2 Chronicles 35:21-24)

Doing special things for God didn't give Josiah license to do whatever he wanted to do. The same is true of us. We can't be presumptuous! We must not go into battle against God's command. Even if we are doing great things in the Lord, we are not indispensable, nor immortal, nor indestructible.

KEEP PERSPECTIVE IN THE BATTLE

Having looked at these battle strategies, we need to give some thought to maintaining our perspective in spiritual warfare. The first key to doing so is understanding that we don't have to be afraid. It is true that the devil is a formidable enemy, one whose malice and destructive power we must never underestimate nor disregard. But it is also true that God has fully armed us for battle. While we must not look for trouble by seeking out opportunities to confront the devil and forces of evil, we can be prepared to face them as they arise. If we are ever confronted by the forces of evil, we can experience the calm confidence that comes from the peace, power, and presence of God. Countless believers testify to this.

The second key to maintaining perspective is staying balanced. Fascination with spiritual warfare has lured many people into strange and even destructive situations. There is a side of human nature that is magnetically lured toward the darkness. I know of a man who taught extensively on spiritual warfare, going deeper and deeper into the subject. Losing sight of the world and the flesh as sources of sin, he saw all evil as being caused directly by the devil and the demonic. He even began to dabble in the study of witchcraft "in order to better defeat it," he said. But something went terribly wrong. His life disintegrated on every level: his personal commitment to Christ, his marriage, his family, and his ministry. Consequently, many who had been initially helped by his insights into spiritual warfare became afraid or skeptical. This is not an uncommon story.

It is very easy to look for a scapegoat or quick fix by focusing too soon and too often on the demonic. While the demonic is real, we would do well to examine evil first on the plane of the flesh and the world before considering the possibility of demonic interference.

Instead of studying evil, therefore, we should study spiritual health and holiness. God is shaping a victorious people, citizens of his kingdom. We must know the nature of the enemy, but even more we must know our blessings and responsibilities in God's kingdom.

I once heard a doctor say that one of the biggest mistakes we make is to study disease more than we study health. "You can study what is wrong forever and never study what you need to do to keep healthy," she said. "We could fill all the books in the world with descriptions of disease, but we can put the principles for a healthy life on a three-by-five-inch card!" In keeping with this wisdom, let's conclude our study by reminding ourself of the principles for spiritual health:

• Give your absolute allegiance to the Lord through faith, commitment, and godly living.

- Live a life characterized by confession, repentance, and Spirit-enabled obedience.
- Rely on God's grace for forgiveness and for daily living.
- Understand and stand under God's Word through the renewal of your mind and the development of a biblical worldview.
- Live in authentic Christian community.
- Exercise your spiritual gifts in God's service.
- Exercise your authority in Christ.
- Recognize that you're in a spiritual battle and that you must protect yourself through the whole armor of God.
- Use your vast repertoire of prayers and ministry tools.

As we do these things, relying on the grace and power of God the Father, God the Son, and God the Holy Spirit, we will see the victory of the Lord and his coming kingdom.

Martin Luther lived with a vivid sense of the devil and spiritual warfare. His stirring hymn, "A Mighty Fortress Is Our God," based on Psalm 46 and translated from German by Frederick H. Hedge, expressed the confidence we all can have:

> *A mighty fortress is our God,*
> *A bulwark never failing;*
> *Our helper He amid the flood*
> *Of mortal ills prevailing.*
> *For still our ancient foe*

Doth seek to work us woe—
His craft and pow'r are great,
And armed with cruel hate,
On earth is not His equal.

Did we in our own strength confide,
Our striving would be losing,
Were not the right man on our side,
The man of God's own choosing;
Dost ask who that may be?
Christ Jesus, it is He—
Lord Sabaoth His name,
From age to age the same,
And He must win the battle.

And tho' this world, with devils filled,
Should threaten to undo us,
We will not fear, for God hath willed
His truth to triumph through us.
The prince of darkness grim,
We tremble not for him—
His rage we can endure,
For lo! his doom is sure:
One little word shall fell him.

That word above all earthly pow'rs,
No thanks to them, abideth;
The Spirit and the gifts are ours
Through Him who with us sideth.
Let goods and kindred go,
This mortal life also—

> *The body they may kill;*
> *God's truth abideth still:*
> *His kingdom is forever.*

From *The One Year Book of Hymns* (Wheaton, Ill.: Tyndale House Publishers, Inc., 1995), October 31.

The term *Sabaoth* does not refer to the Sabbath, as many mistakenly assume, but is the Hebrew word for "hosts" or "armies" of heaven. When our resources are feeble, it helps us to remember that the Lord is commander of the hosts of heaven and earth. As Jesus said in Matthew 26:53, "Don't you realize that I could ask my Father for thousands of angels to protect us, and he would send them instantly?" In the original Greek, the number of angels is referred to as twelve legions. A legion was a Roman battle group of soldiers numbering six thousand. So Jesus was saying that God could instantly send seventy-two thousand angels! How can we not be impressed with the scope of God's power? Through his Word, through angels, through the power of the Holy Spirit, and ultimately through the risen, reigning Lord, God comes against evil. We are part of his army, equipped with his armor and his Spirit.

At the heart of the matter, spiritual warfare is not really Satan's war against us, but God's war against evil. God has enlisted us in the battle so that we will be victors in him.

Be strong and take courage. The battle is the Lord's!

ABOUT THE AUTHOR

Dr. Douglas J. Rumford has pastored congregations for over twenty-one years, most recently as senior pastor of First Presbyterian Church, Fresno, California. He previously served congregations in Old Greenwich, Connecticut, and Fairfield, Connecticut. Now acquisitions director for nonfiction books at Tyndale House Publishers, Doug continues to speak frequently at conferences and churches.

Doug is the author of several books, including *SoulShaping* and *Questions God Asks, Questions Satan Asks,* both published by Tyndale House. Doug has also written a number of articles for such publications as *New Man* magazine, *Moody* magazine, *Christianity Today,* and *Leadership* journal.

Doug received his doctor of ministry degree from Fuller Theological Seminary. He earned his master of divinity degree from Gordon-Conwell Theological Seminary, graduating *summa cum laude* as valedictorian of his class, and a bachelor of arts degree from Miami University, Oxford, Ohio.

Doug and his wife, Sarah, have been married twenty-five years and have four children. Doug's goal in ministry is to touch hearts and minds with the truth, grace, and power of God: "As I serve Jesus Christ, my greatest joy is bringing ideas to life that can change lives."